THE BEASTS OF NEVER

The Beasts

A HISTORY NATURAL & UNNATURAL

# of Never

OF MONSTERS MYTHICAL & MAGICAL

by GEORGESS McHARGUE

Illustrated by FRANK BOZZO

Revised and Expanded Edition

Delacorte
Press

This book is for Nancy
in memory of our monstrous childhood
and for my parents who lived through it.

Published by
Delacorte Press
The Bantam Doubleday Dell Publishing Group, Inc.
1 Dag Hammarskjold Plaza
New York, New York 10017

Text copyright © 1968, 1988 by Georgess McHargue
Illustrations copyright © 1968 by Frank Bozzo

Library of Congress Cataloging in Publication Data
McHargue, Georgess.
The beasts of never.

Bibliography: p.
Includes index.
Summary: Traces the history of many imaginary creatures as they have
appeared in myth and legend through the ages, describes their different
species and characteristics, gives possible sources of their legendary ori-
gin, and offers explanations for supposed sightings by man.
1. Animals, Mythical—Juvenile literature. [1. Animals, Mythical]
I. Bozzo, Frank, ill. II. Title.
GR825.M269   1987   398'.4   86-29374
ISBN 0-385-29573-1

Manufactured in the United States of America

June 1988
10 9 8 7 6 5 4 3 2 1
BG

PREFACE

THIS book is the first in a series of four in which I hope to revive some of the old lore about Dragons, Unicorns, Werewolves, Witches, Gardens of Paradise, Floating Islands, Seven League Boots, and Invincible Swords. These things are not "factual" as we would define the word, but they were still entirely *real* to their creators. *The Beasts of Never* first appeared in 1968, and this new edition contains much material that refers to recent events or discoveries in archaeology and folklore. It is concerned with the history, natural and unnatural, of fabulous animals. *The Impossible People* (1972) dealt with beings of human and half-human ancestry; *The Lands of Elsewhere* will be about mythical geography; and *Things of Power* will cover magic objects. In each case I have emphasized beliefs and traditions of western Europe, because that is the area which has contributed most to our poetry, history, and art. Yet the magical beasts, personages, lands, and objects of Africa, Asia, and the Americas are equally fascinating, sometimes for their strangeness, sometimes for their striking similarities to those of European origin, and by including them I have hoped to show that in their hopes and fears, and especially in their soaring imaginations, all the peoples of the world are one.

G. McH.
1987

TABLE OF CONTENTS

LIST OF ILLUSTRATIONS

INTRODUCTION

E V E R since human beings first learned to talk, people have been telling each other tales and stories.
Around the campfire or through the long winter eve-
nings, the storytellers have drawn about themselves a
circle of listening faces. Sometimes the tales were
true, the teller's own adventures. But often the
speaker was carried away and told what might have
happened, or what should have happened. Many
times, people used stories to explain natural events
they could not otherwise understand. It was easy to
imagine that the waning moon was eaten each month
by some greedy monster, or that earthquakes were
the movements of huge creatures underground.

In ways like these were born tales of fabulous
beasts that never really walked or ran or slithered
upon this earth. In time the reality of these legends
became accepted because it was part of tradition. If
you had not seen the beasts yourself, your cousin
knew a man who said he had. And who would doubt
it? The world was so full of wonders that new things
were always turning up.

Sometimes, too, a real animal became the basis for
a legend because those who had seen it could not find
the right words to tell the tale. How, for example,
would you describe a bear or an elephant to someone
who had never seen one? You could easily give your
listener some very odd ideas of the beast, particularly
if you were not sure of the details yourself.

Soon, therefore, the folk tales, the legends, and the

epics of the world became filled with Dragons, Unicorns, Griffins, Sea Monsters, and other wonders. They were carved and painted and drawn, written and sung about. The people of medieval times were as well acquainted with the Phoenix as with the lion.

Nowadays, however, many of us have lost touch with the wonderful beasts of the past. We know they are not real, that one cannot count their teeth or measure their blood pressure. And so, though we hear about them in fairy tales and see them carved on ancient buildings, we ignore them. Few people now can tell the story of the Phoenix, or describe the Unicorn correctly, or defend themselves against the Basilisk, if they should be unlucky enough to meet one.

Yet these imaginary animals, these beasts of never, have a real importance, and this is not merely because they are part of history and legend. It is because they are truly magic. By this I mean that the people who invented them were expressing their own hopes and fears. In doing so, they made their fears less terrible and their wishes more possible. The person who first told of the winged horse Pegasus had created a creature that *ought* to be—a stallion swift and beautiful and tireless, whose shining wings would carry his rider ever higher, beyond the noise and dust of the everyday world. That is more like true magic than anything done by a wizard with a wand or a scientist with lenses and test tubes.

THE BEASTS OF NEVER

The Dragon Foul and Fell

The old Dragon under ground
In straiter limits bound
Not half so far casts his usurped sway
And wroth to see his kingdom fail
Swinges the scaly horrour of his folded tail.

MILTON

ABOVE the pleasant meadow, where the rocks begin, a dark thread of smoke hangs in the air. Though the silence is touched now by a faint sound, the mouth of the great cavern in the hillside is empty. Or, as the noise of hoofs grows louder, do two sparks of yellow fire wink once in the hollow hole?

Suddenly the challenge of a horn is heard, and a knight rides into view. The steel blue of his armor flashes across the field. The shining surcoat ripples in the wind of his charge. Behind him hasten the inhabitants of the nearby town—shopkeepers and children, dogs and donkeys, women with babes in arms.

But the watchers halt in terror at the edge of the field, for now there is a hot glow in the cave mouth and their quarry is in sight. It is the Dragon, ancient, fierce, and cruel.

Out it springs in one great leap, beating the air with its webby wings. But before it can leap again, the warrior on the white horse has driven his spear deep between the beetle-green scales of the Dragon's neck.

Now the battle is joined in earnest. With drawn sword the knight seeks to hack off the fearful head of his enemy. Valiantly the great charger rears and side-steps, using teeth and hoofs to ward off the blows of steely claws and scaly tail. Forgotten now are the wrongs of the villagers, the stolen cattle, imprisoned maidens, ruined farmsteads. The hero who dared adventure his strength and courage in the cause of justice is fighting for his life, and the grass is black with blood. Gathering all his strength, he lets fall a blow like a thunderbolt.

It is done. Slowly the terrible creature collapses in a sprawl of scales and a hiss of scorching breath. With a cheer the villagers rush forward to marvel at the dead monster and praise their deliverer. He is the Dragon slayer; there will be peace in the land again.

Is he Saint George or Sir Lancelot? It hardly matters, for the tale has been told of many thousand heroes. In various forms this oldest of monster stories has made itself a permanent part of folklore around the world. If it were not for the Dragon, there would hardly be any fairy tales—no beautiful princesses rescued by handsome princes, no magic swords, no golden treasure won, and, worst of all, nobody living happily ever after. The Dragon is the most nearly universal character in all folklore, except the child who is left to die in the wilderness.

But what do we really know of the Dragon? True, it is very big and very fierce, but so is a tiger. What is it that makes a Dragon a Dragon, and not a Sea Serpent, a Griffin, a whale? How does it look, how long does it live, where did it come from, how does it act? Most people today could not begin to answer these questions. The Dragon, they will say, does not *exist.* By this they mean that you cannot see a Dragon in a zoo, and that is certainly so. But such a statement is not at all the same as saying a creature is not *real.* If you have ever been frightened by the grinding growl of a thunderstorm or the crackling flash of lightning out of nowhere, the Dragon is real for you in something like the same way it was real for the first tellers of tales thousands of years ago. The Dragon, you see, was as real as people's fear of it, as real as their wish to escape its wrath, as real as the lives of those who believed in it. For this reason, as well as for the sake of cheerful curiosity, it is worthwhile for us to ask questions about mythical creatures—the answers may tell us something about the way the human mind works and about the growth and development of ideas.

In speaking of Dragons, it must be made clear that there are in the family at least two different species which will have to be considered separately. First, there is the familiar Dragon of European fairy tales— a fierce, greedy, and wicked monster. Then there is the Dragon of the Orient, who may look like its western cousin but who has entirely different habits, being generally of a kind and helpful nature. The two are so unlike each other that this chapter will be devoted entirely to the western Dragon, leaving the eastern Dragon for Chapter II.

In the Mediterranean world, where western civilization began, the Dragon is certainly older than the first recorded history. It is evidently the first, the worst, the supreme monster.

In the earliest tales and pictures (three, four, or even five thousand years old), the Dragon clearly represents storm clouds and rain, some of the most important and primitive elements in nature. The sun is

*The Dragon
Foul and Fell*

· · · · · ·

5

FIERY EYE

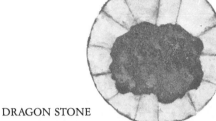

DRAGON STONE

MAGICAL HEART

the bringer of light and warmth, but water, in the form of rainfall or of flooding rivers like the Nile, the Tigris, and the Indus, is the bringer of crops and the renewer of life. Without the annual rains, fields are barren, animals sicken, and people starve. Thus the Dragon of the storm clouds is a mighty creature who guards a treasure greater than gold or silver. And when it withholds its store of rain for weeks or months at a time, there is cause for real alarm. Then sometimes the people pray and make sacrifices (perhaps of beautiful maidens), hoping to appease the Dragon's anger. And it may happen that, in answer to their prayers, the storm breaks and the swollen, slate-purple clouds overhead let down the long-awaited rain. Then the people say that the sky god, with his sword of lightning and hammer of thunder, has conquered the Dragon and freed them from fear.

Everywhere in the countries of Europe and the Mediterranean, this story appears in one form or another. The name of the hero and the circumstances of the battle may differ, but in the background of a thousand myths we can see this same episode played out again and again for the benefit of fearful people who were at the mercy of the weather.

Just what was the western Dragon like? Actually, by the medieval period, there were two distinct types of Dragon in the West. One was the huge, scaly, but legless Wurm, with a poisonous breath and the ability to join itself together again if cut in two. Wurms are

The Beasts of Never

. . . .

6

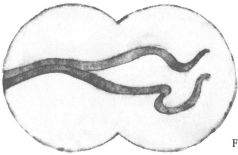

most common in the tales of northern Europe, particularly among peoples whose native languages belong to the Celtic or Germanic family. The other type of Dragon is the one we most commonly bring to mind —the creature with webby wings, spikes down its back, two or four legs, and fiery breath. This latter Dragon is heraldic; that is, its appearance is derived from the way it was shown on medieval coats of arms. Both kinds appear in folk tales, where Wurms are somewhat longer but heraldic Dragons are swifter in the attack.

As for size, the best classical sources say that a full-grown Dragon may be up to one hundred fifty feet long. Dragons may be of any color, but the most usual seems to be green—either a poisonous metallic color or a sickly blackish hue. Their bodies are covered with tough, shining scales that, often, can be pierced by a weapon at only one vital point, such as the throat or the precise middle of the back. The tail is long and coiling, and in heraldic Dragons may end in a barb or poisonous sting. When there are wings, they often join the body behind the forelegs.

The Dragon's head is truly fearsome. Whether or not it has horns, it certainly has great bulging eyes, a long snout, and a set of dreadfully efficient teeth. The tongue is usually forked or barbed, regardless of whether the Dragon is of the fire-breathing or venom-dripping variety.

In addition to these outward appearances, there are

The Dragon
Foul and Fell

7

some less obvious facts about the Dragon that it would be useful for the ambitious Dragon slayer to know. For one thing, anybody who eats a Dragon's heart will acquire the ability to speak all the languages of the earth, both human and animal. Second, there is inside the Dragon's head or in its forehead a magical stone that will cure almost any illness and gives wonderful powers to the owner. There is only one difficulty about acquiring this stone: one must not injure the Dragon. Since there are very few people who would try to sneak up on a sleeping Dragon, it is easy to understand why there are not many specimens of these stones. About the only way to get a sample is to find one which has been accidentally dropped by a Dragon as it flies overhead.

As has been said, Dragons are found all over the world and may live anywhere, but their favorite haunts are swamps and mountain caves. That they like swamps is easily explained when one remembers their association with water, but their taste for caves needs to be discussed a little further. It turns out that the Dragon is not only a storm demon but the ruler of the underground. This sovereignty is perhaps connected to its first role, for the storm clouds often seem to come up over the horizon, and where can they have come from but under the earth? So it seemed to primitive peoples, at any rate. Furthermore, in areas of the world where there were earthquakes and volcanic eruptions it was natural to suppose that the thunder and fires in the sky must be related to the thunder and fires underground. Thus the Dragon was blamed for both occurrences. The Dragon became, in fact, so closely associated with the underworld that in Christian times it has often been confused with the Devil, although the Prince of Darkness, in his present form, is a newcomer to the scene of folklore, compared with the Dragon.

The European Dragon has only two proper occupations: guarding treasure and devouring maidens. In the course of these two activities the Dragon also lays waste the countryside, trampling and scorching crops, stealing cattle, destroying property, and the like. It must take a great deal to feed a one-hundred-fifty-foot reptile. Perhaps the Dragon's large food requirement explains why there is seldom more than one Dragon at a time in a story. A whole herd of the monsters would simply starve to death in any area smaller than a kingdom.

For a closer look at the habits of Dragons, the best method will be to make the acquaintance of a few individual members of the clan and see how they fared in various countries and times.

Certainly one of the oldest Dragons on record is Tiamat, a female monster who appears in the legends of the Babylonians of about 2000 B.C. Tiamat, it is told, was of such vast size that no one could measure her bulk. In the days before the creation of the world, she rebelled against the gods in an effort to keep the universe in a perpetual state of darkness and chaos. But the sun god, Marduk, forged weapons with which to subdue her—bow, sword, net, storm winds, and lightning bolt. After a fearful battle at which the whole universe trembled, Marduk slew Tiamat and hacked her body into two pieces, one of which formed the heavens and the other the earth. This legend was written down on cuneiform tablets about four thousand years ago, but it must have been current as a myth long before that.

Very similar is the Hindu myth of the slaying of the Dragon Vrtra by Indra, whose weapon was the thunderbolt. In this tale, first recorded in the Hindu holy books called the Vedas, over three thousand years ago, the name *Vrtra* means obstruction, and the heroism of Indra brings about the release of the captive waters of heaven. Thus in two of the oldest Dragon stories known to us, the connection of the Dragon with storms and water is already well established.

Among classical Dragon stories, by far the best known, and the model for countless variations, is the Greek one of Perseus and Andromeda. Though not

divine himself, as Marduk was, Perseus was a son of the sky god Zeus. The young man already had established himself as a hero by the time he rescued Andromeda, having earlier slain the Gorgon Medusa. In any case, Perseus happened to be passing through the domain of King Cepheus just at the right time. Cassiopeia, the king's wife, had been so rash as to claim that her beauty was greater than that of the Nereids, daughters of the sea god Poseidon. In punishment Poseidon sent a great flood to ruin the land and a monster to devour the people. An oracle informed Cepheus and Cassiopeia that the anger of Poseidon would be satisfied if they would sacrifice their daughter Andromeda to the monster. For the sake of his people, Cepheus was forced to agree, and the lovely Andromeda was already chained to the tide-washed rock when Perseus appeared. Drawing his sword, he barred the way of the advancing Dragon and there followed a terrible battle which turned the waves red with blood. At last, though, the Dragon was vanquished (sons of Zeus do not come off second best in this kind of contest) and the victor was able to claim the maiden for his wife.

Perseus, it appears, accomplished his great feat without the aid of magical weapons or spells, which was clever of him and rather unusual. Not until the time of the Christian saints, who were armored by their faith alone, were there to be many others who relied solely upon a strong right arm in such a battle.

The greatest experts in magical Dragon slaying

were the heroes of Norse and German legend. To them, swords tempered in Dragon's blood, cloaks of invisibility, invulnerable armor, and secret spells were merely tools of the trade. In these northern tales the Dragons, too, seem to have changed a little. Some now live ninety years underground, ninety years in the branches of a lime tree, and ninety years in the desert. Furthermore, the eating of maidens is no longer a common occupation. Northern Dragons focus instead on hoarding gold. An example of this type of Dragon is Fafnir, who was eventually slain by the Germanic hero Siegfried. Fafnir began his career as an ordinary giant, but after he had acquired the cursed Rhine treasure in payment for some work done for the god Odin, he became so consumed with miserliness that he turned into a Dragon, the better to guard and gloat over his hoard.

The wickedness of Dragons is not invariable, however. There is at least one tale of a tame one. A little Greek boy, so the Roman naturalist Pliny tells us, once found a baby Dragon, brought it home, and fed it. Unfortunately, the boy's parents, like so many other parents then and now, were not pleased with his choice of a pet. Ignoring his son's protests, the father took the friendly little beast into the desert and abandoned it. Many years later, when the boy had become a grown man, he was set upon by bandits while making a journey in a far land. Suddenly a great Dragon came roaring out of the thickets and frightened the thieves away. It was, of course, the same Dragon, and the man and his former pet had a happy reunion.

The tale of the friendly Dragon is a pleasant relief from the usual run of Dragon stories, which tend to follow the same predictable pattern of hero meets Dragon, hero slays Dragon, hero wins maiden. While most Dragons are decidedly *not* friendly, it is not always necessary to be a Perseus, a Siegfried, or a Saint George in order to eliminate one. There are at least four methods for doing away with unwanted monsters which do not call for physical combat, and some of them are so ingenious as to be downright unsportsmanlike.

Method Number One was practiced in its best-known form by a Greek named Menestratus. This resourceful fellow went to a blacksmith and had made for himself a suit of armor covered at every point with spikes and fishhooks. Then, strolling calmly into the Dragon's lair, he allowed himself to be swallowed up. The unfortunate monster shortly died of indigestion, allowing its clever killer to hack his way out of the carcass unharmed. This approach to Dragon slaying became quite popular, and appears in legends from parts as distant as Ireland and France and in the American Indian tale of the slaying of Mashenomak.

Method Number Two was also used over a wide geographical area. In the ancient city of Babylon, as some versions of the Bible tell, the prophet Daniel came before King Nebuchadnezzar with an offer to rid the city of a Dragon which the people were worshiping and supplying with victims. Daniel promised to kill the beast without drawing a sword, as proof that the God of the Hebrews was stronger than the evil god represented by the Dragon. Having received the King's permission to try, Daniel concocted a ball of pitch and other materials which he then fed to the hungry monster. This indigestible tidbit presently caused the Dragon to burst in pieces, adding greatly to Daniel's reputation as a wonder worker. This same technique was used by Cracus, the legendary founder of the Polish city of Krakow. Cracus is supposed to have used sulfur for his fatal pill, and the tale says that it exploded when the Dragon went to drink.

Of the third method there is only one known example, which, though it seems a little treacherous, was certainly effective. At Deerhurst, England, during the Middle Ages, a man named John Smith volunteered to rid the neighborhood of a troublesome Dragon. He then left a large quantity of milk in a place where the monster was accustomed to walk. The Dragon saw the milk, gulped it down, and stretched itself out on the ground for a nap, as the story says, "with his scales ruffled up." Smith took advantage of the Dragon in its moment of relaxation and struck it with a sword in between its ruffled scales. Thus perished another foul menace.

Method Number Four can only be practiced by a saint, and thus is not much good for everyday use. Nevertheless, it was often successful in early Christian times when saints were plentiful. Saint George of Cappadocia had set the best-known pattern for Dragon slaying in the conventional way, having attacked from horseback armed with spear and sword. Saint Martha, however, used an entirely different approach. The people of Nerluc, France, called upon her to aid them against a Dragon named Tarasque, who was preying on travelers. The good saint betook herself to the monster's den and tamed it by sprinkling it with holy water. Then, leashing the beast with her sash, she led it into the central square of Nerluc, where the cheering townspeople slaughtered it without mercy. It is hard not to feel that the poor Dragon was unfairly treated, even though the town was later renamed Tarascon in its honor. A similar deed was performed at Rouen, France, by St. Romain, about A.D. 520.

Just about the last report of a really genuine Dragon was made in A.D. 1330. At that time, on the Mediterranean island of Rhodes, people claimed to have seen a fearful beast the size of a horse. It had a long neck, a serpent's head, mule's ears, a gaping mouth full of teeth, flashing eyes, four feet with bear-like claws, a tail like a crocodile's, scales, and wings. The upper body was blue, while the under parts were red and yellow. The hero who slew this monster was Dieudonné de Gozon. He had other problems to contend with besides fighting the Dragon, for he was one of the Knights of Saint John, a military-religious organization which enforced strict discipline. De Gozon's superior forbade him to waste time in Dragon slaying, so the Knight was forced to make preparations in secret. He set up a paper Dragon in his backyard and trained his horse and dogs to attack it fearlessly. By this means he was able to overcome the Dragon without difficulty. Unfortunately, De Gozon did not have such an easy time with his superior, who had him thrown into jail for disobedience. It was a long way from the times when such a deed might have won a man a kingdom.

After this event Dragons began a steady decline in quantity and quality. Within a couple of centuries the poor monsters became so reduced that on May 18, 1572, a simple Italian cowherd named Baptista killed a hissing Dragon near Bologna merely by knocking it on the head. One might say that this was the death blow of the European Dragon. People had ceased to believe in it, and so it disappeared.

Now that we have met the Dragon of myth and learned something of its habits and history, we may

ask whether there is any way of explaining this fabulous monster. Is there anything in the history of myth-making (which scholars call mythography) or in the appearance and habits of real animals that may have formed the basis for the legend?

With regard to the meaning of the Dragon in myth, its connection with water, storms, and the underworld, and its habit of hoarding treasure have already been discussed. One may still wonder, however, why it is that Dragons spend so much of their time devouring (or threatening to devour) maidens.

In mythology there are rarely any simple or obvious answers to such questions. We may guess, however, that the habit of eating maidens may go back to a time when actual human sacrifice was offered to the storm demon. In such a situation the girl could only be "saved" by the intervention of the sky hero with his lightning sword. Another possibility is that the maiden in the story is the moon goddess, for the moon is often associated with water in mythology because of its connection with the tides of the sea. Thus the storm clouds hiding the moon may have been thought of as the Dragon holding the goddess captive.

But was there ever, anywhere, a real Dragon? As we have seen, there were reports of live Dragons as recently as a few hundred years ago. And some people still think a monster so marvelous and so universal could not be pure invention.

The Dragon
Foul and Fell

15

Naturally, as soon as we look for a real Dragon, we think of the dinosaurs. Judging from the fossil remains of these giant creatures, they would have made very convincing Dragons, since some of them possessed both great size and frightful ferocity. Unfortunately, geology shows us that it is utterly impossible that any human being, no matter how primitive, was alive during the age of the dinosaurs, which were thoroughly extinct millions of years before the evolution of the first creature that could call itself human.

But if we must do without living dinosaurs as a source of the Dragon legends, we may at least make use of their fossil bones. Fossils were easy to find in many parts of the world in ancient times, and their enormous size certainly contributed to tales of both Dragons and Giants.

Among living animals of the western world, it seems clear that the most direct "ancestor" of the Dragon was some sort of large snake, probably the Indian python. This member of the constrictor family may reach a length of thirty feet, likes to lie in forest pools, and sometimes makes its home in caves, all of which sounds much like the Dragon. A very ancient carving of Tiamat, the Babylonian chaos Dragon, shows her simply as a snake with legs. The idea that the Dragon of the West is more snake than anything else is further borne out by the fact that in many languages the words for snake and Dragon are the same, and by the popularity of the Wurm variety of Dragon in Europe.

Other contributors to the shape of the Dragon are not hard to find: the larger lizards, the venomous

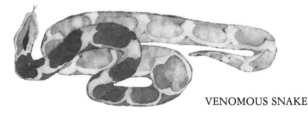

VENOMOUS SNAKE

snakes, and the crocodile probably all gave something to the finished creation.

So there it stands—storm demon, python, lizard, nightmare. As a farewell to the Dragon, now that it is no more, one cannot do better than to look at it through the eyes of a Hebrew commentator of A.D. 1035, who wrote in an expanded version of the Book of Job:

> Where wast thou in the day when I formed the dragon? His food is in the sea and his dwelling is in the air; his eyes flash fire; his ears are like the bow of the clouds, there pours forth from them flames as though he were a whirling column of dust; his belly burns and his breath flames forth in hot coals like unto rocks; it is as though the clash of his teeth were sounds of thunder and the glance of his eye were the flashing of lightning; armies pass him by while he is lying; nothing terrifies him; in him there is no joint . . . he destroys all that by which he passes.

It is a fitting tribute to the greatest monster of them all.

Dragon Kings II
of the East

The small dragon is a caterpillar;
the large dragon fills heaven and earth.
CHINESE SAYING

IN the Orient, as well as in the western world, the Dragon is supreme among mythical beasts. It is the chief of the Four Benevolent Creatures, the others being the Phoenix, the Unicorn, and the Tortoise. The habits and disposition of the eastern Dragon are very different from those of its western cousin, although the two look much alike to a casual eye. Like ancient China itself, Chinese Dragons are highly civilized. They are not solitary and wicked demons devastating the countryside, but members of an elaborate Dragon kingdom organized on the same lines as the real kingdom ruled by the Emperor.

Dragons served a very important purpose in Chinese life. It was they who had charge of all the waterways, all the streams and rivers, all ponds, lakes, and oceans, and all rainfall. It was their task, therefore, to see that the crops would grow and that the rivers would stay between their banks and not overflow in the disastrous floods that have so often brought famine and death to that part of the world. In carrying out their duties as water wardens, the Dragons were usually benevolent, though sometimes vain and unreliable. They were organized into several departments, each with particular duties. If there was too much or too little rainfall, the Chinese people knew precisely which Dragons were to blame and how to register a complaint in proper form. If, for example, the Cloud Dragon had neglected to send any rain for the fields, the people might put its image in the town jail, scolding and berating it as if the Dragon were a common criminal. Legend says that this sort of treatment often worked. Certainly it was not the habit of Chinese Dragons to demand tender maidens as the price of their cooperation.

Oriental Dragons share a tradition of great wealth with the western ones, as well as an association with water. The Dragon kings in their underwater palaces were fabulously rich, and what is more, they were usually generous to human beings who were lucky enough to stumble into their domains.

A Japanese tale tells of Tawara Toda, a warrior said to have lived in the eleventh century. One night Toda was crossing a bridge when he saw lying upon it a huge and hideous serpent. Ignoring the monster, he went calmly on his way. Later that night, a beautiful young girl visited him at his home. She praised the courage he had shown at the bridge and revealed that the serpent was herself in another form and that she was the daughter of the Dragon King. She begged Toda to help her people by slaying a monstrous centipede that was threatening them.

Toda destroyed the centipede, and as a reward the Dragon princess took him to visit the palace of her father, which lay beneath the waters of a lake. There he was entertained with every kind of delicacy that grows in the water, from baked carp to water chestnuts, and given three magical parting gifts: a sacred bell from India, a bale of rice that could never be used up, and a roll of silk cloth that never ran out. Toda piously hung the bell in a lakeside temple and kept the other two gifts for himself, so that in all his later adventures (and they were many) he was always well fed and well clothed.

In addition to treasure, anyone who entered a Dragon palace would find a truly remarkable-looking creature. The Chinese Dragon is traditionally described in the following way: It has a camel's head, deer's horns, rabbit's eyes, cow's ears, snake's neck, frog's belly, carp's scales, hawk's claws, and tiger's palms. This does not really give an accurate idea of the monster's appearance, however, for over the centuries Chinese artists came to draw the Dragon in a way that fitted the elaborate designs of their pottery, embroidery, and carving. The animal that the artists finally developed is a masterpiece of writhing coils and snakelike curves. Its long-snouted head with bulging eyes is ornamented with horns and whiskers, its four legs strut proudly and show their claws, and its tail is finished off with an elegant cluster of spikes.

Among Dragons the number of claws is a symbol of rank. The Dragon Emperor has five claws on each foot, while the lesser grades have four or three. Likewise, a Dragon's color may be azure, green, red, black, white, or yellow, depending on its place in the Dragon organization. Its whole appearance is much more variable than the western Dragon's. It may be dark, bright, or invisible at will. In addition, it can assume the shape of a bird or a human being. It is deaf, and its voice is like the jingling of copper coins.

In many of its pictures the Chinese Dragon is

shown reaching for a round ball in front of it. The nature of this ball has given rise to a great deal of discussion. It has been taken for the sun or a thunderbolt, but the best interpretation seems to be that it is a combined symbol for the moon and a pearl. This would fit nicely with the watery nature of the dragon. In China, as everywhere else, the tides are controlled largely by the moon. Moreover, the pearl is traditionally the jewel of the moon, both because it is round and white and because it comes from the sea. Perhaps, therefore, the original treasure of the Oriental Dragon was a hoard of pearls, tiny sacred moons lighting the dim, watery halls of the Dragon's palace.

All over China, the tale-tellers say, Dragons have left visible signs of their existence. Fossils were known from earliest times as Dragon bones, and the red-streaked ore called cinnabar was supposed to contain Dragon's blood. In early times, too, glass was thought to be the crystallized breath of the Dragon, which on other occasions might appear either as rain or as fire. In mountain streams one could find the beautiful round pebbles that were Dragon's eggs. When ready to hatch, they split open during a thunderstorm, and the young Dragons leapt up to the sky. Once, so they say, a young Dragon failed in its leap and fell back to earth. The Emperor happened to witness the event and had the little monster killed and made into soup for his chief ministers. The lesson he

The Beasts
of Never

· · · · · · ·

wished to impress on them was clear, for (in Chinese thought) the Dragon's leap symbolized rise to high position. The subtle Emperor was reminding his great lords of the responsibilities of office and the penalties of failure.

Once it has successfully made its way to heaven, as almost all newly hatched Dragons do, the young creature grows rapidly and soon becomes adult. Full-grown Dragons have an immense appetite for swallows, the little birds being their favorite food. So great is this passion of theirs that persons who have eaten swallows for dinner are well advised not to cross a bridge or go near water, lest the resident Dragon be carried away by the nearness of swallows and gulp them down alive. Dragons have another peculiarity also: they are easily frightened by centipedes or by a piece of silk dyed with five colors.

The Dragon kingdom is divided into four principal departments, each ruled by its own Dragon King. The Dragons known as *t'ien-lung* guard and support the mansions of the gods. The *shen-lung* bring rain and wind. The *ti-lung* are in charge of rivers and streams, and the *fu-ts'ang-lung* are the guardians of hidden treasure.

The history of the Dragon in China goes back to very ancient times indeed. In literature there are references to it as early as 2700 B.C., at which time the legend was by no means new. From the facts already related it will be plain that the eastern and western Dragons are much alike, and many scholars believe that the two have a common origin. If that is so, the place from which both Dragons came was probably India, which is situated between East and West, and which has been a center of cultural influence since prehistoric times.

The legends of India are crowded with gods, demons, and strange beasts. Among these one may find a group of beings called Nagas. They were basically cobra gods, but were able to assume human form at will—a power which, as you will recall, also belongs to the Oriental Dragon, although not to the western one. The history and functions of the Nagas are exceedingly hard to unravel, but it is known that their kings lived at the bottom of lakes or seas, that they were believed to control storms, and that they possessed fabulous treasures of pearls. They were associated with the god Indra, the bringer of rain, slayer of Vrtra. Thus it seems plausible that the Nagas (and, through them, the Indian cobra) were to some extent responsible for the development of the Dragon in the East, and possibly in the West as well. It is interesting to note that the Indian Naga legends do not feature the slaying of Nagas by sun gods or heroes. It may be that that part of the Dragon legend is principally a western invention. That would explain why the Chinese Dragon came in general to represent the life-

The Beasts
of Never

. . . .

24

NAGA

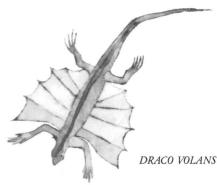

DRACO VOLANS

MAKARA

giving properties of water, while the western one was associated with its terrifying or destructive aspects.

There is another creature in Indian legend that may have played a part in spawning the Dragon. It is called the Makara, and Hindu legend makes the Makara the steed of the water god Varuna. It is impossible to describe the Makara accurately, for it has a multitude of forms. The one thing that can always be said of it is that it has a fishtail. In its forepart it may look like a goat, cat, elephant, or just about anything else. At other times the Makara has the legs of an antelope, piglike ears and snout, and scales, in addition to the fishtail.

In some of its pictures the Makara bears a surprising resemblance to the bottle-nosed dolphin, while in others it looks more like the crocodile, a reptile found in the rivers of southern China and India. This Makara-crocodile may have given the Oriental Dragon its four legs and spiky tail, as well as its taste for swallows. It happens that the crocodile is often seen in the company of a species of small bird which picks off irritating parasites from the big reptile's skin, and even from between its teeth. Human observers might easily be deceived into supposing that the crocodile was devouring the birds rather than receiving free dental service. It is hard to believe that any creature would willingly walk into those enormous jaws.

In our search for the eastern Dragon's "ancestors,"

Dragon Kings of the East

· · · · · · ·

25

we have to consider two real creatures that are not connected with legend, as the cobra and crocodile are. The first is a little lizard that lives in Java. Its Latin name is *Draco volans,* which means flying dragon, and fly it does, after a fashion. Between the fore and hind legs its body is extended sideways by a series of false ribs covered by a web of skin. This arrangement enables it to "fly" by gliding from one tree to another, much as the American flying squirrel does. The little *Draco volans* is far too insignificant to have played much part in the formation of monster legends, but some writers have suggested that it may have introduced to the people of the East the idea of airborne yet wingless Dragons. As the quotation at the head of this chapter indicates, Dragons were thought to come in every possible size, although the saying was intended more in a philosophical than in a factual sense.

The second real creature that comes into the discussion of Dragon history is perhaps the closest thing to a live Dragon that can be found on this planet today. It is *Varanus komodoensis,* or the Komodo dragon, a large lizard whose existence was unknown until 1912 when it was found living on the island of Komodo in Indonesia. *Varanus komodoensis* is a rather nightmarish creature in its own right, without the help of legend. In shape it is about the same as any four-legged, long-tailed lizard, with this difference: it may grow to a length of over three meters. Furthermore, it is a meat eater and feeds on animals as large as deer and wild pigs. Although it lacks spikes, horns, and wings, its teeth and claws are adequate for any Dragon. When

CHINESE RIVER CROCODILE

it was first discovered, there were those who insisted that the problem of the origin of Dragons was solved. But the fact is that the Komodo dragon was probably just as little known to the Chinese mythmakers as it was to modern zoologists.

Actually, the Dragon is less easily traced to real animals, historical misunderstandings, and the like than is any other mythical creature. It is the oldest, the first, the most basic monster, and at bottom it is nothing but itself.

Phoenix, Bird of the Sun

Now I will believe
. . . that in Arabia
There is one tree, the phoenix'
throne; one phoenix
at this moment reigning there.
SHAKESPEARE

M O S T people today will tell you when you ask that the Phoenix is "that bird that rises from the ashes." Quite probably, this will be the only thing they can tell you about the fabulous bird. Yet the Phoenix has a story as strange and wonderful as anything in mythology.

To begin with, the Phoenix is unique. This means not only that no other bird is like it, but also that it cannot be rivaled even by another Phoenix. For legend says that in all the world there is never more than one Bird of the Sun at a time. If you should be lucky

Phoenix, Bird
of the Sun

· · · · · ·

enough to see one Phoenix, you have seen them all—past, present, and future. The bird before you would have died a million million deaths before this moment and would have a million times as many lifetimes yet to come, always being reborn, always changing, yet always remaining the same.

The period of the Phoenix' strange life is definitely fixed, although various versions of the legend differ as to just what that period is. It is most commonly given as five hundred years. For all the days of its life the Phoenix lives in a deathless and sorrowless land somewhere in the east, a land never visited by mortals. The Phoenix is a bird of peace. During its five hundred years in paradise it eats no living thing, but feeds on air.

At last, however, weary with the burden of the centuries, the Phoenix leaves its home and flies westward. In the groves of Arabia it loads its wings with rare and aromatic spices—frankincense, cinnamon, and myrrh. Then, flying on, it comes to the coast of Phoenicia (at the eastern end of the Mediterranean), the land that bears its name. In the top of the tallest palm tree it builds a nest of spices, and in the nest it waits through the long night. Just at dawn the Phoenix turns to the east and begins to sing, a song not heard in the world for five hundred years. So sweet is the song that the stars, the earth, and the sun itself stop and listen. Then the first rays of the sunrise strike the nest and set it afire. Still singing, the Phoenix is burned to ashes in this funeral pyre of its own making.

But the death of the Bird of the Sun is not forever. In the ashes there remains a small whitish worm, which grows and develops until, on the third day, a new Phoenix arises on strong, young wings. Reverently, the bird gathers up the ashes of its former self, and sets off westward. A long journey later, the flight ends at the sacred Egyptian city of On-Heliopolis. There, on the altar of the sun, the appropriate funeral rites are celebrated by the priests, and then the young, the only, Phoenix sets out again for its ancestral home in paradise. On this return journey it is accompanied by all the birds of this world, its mortal cousins. The eagle and the goose, the hawk and the sparrow, fly side by side without fear until it is time to turn back at the borders of the immortal country. From that point the Phoenix flies on alone, not to reappear for another half-millennium of human history. Then again it will bring a year of good fortune, of peace for the righteous and death to tyrants.

That is the legend of the Phoenix—the complete legend. For, curiously enough, it is just about all we know of the immortal bird. Its appearances in other tales are few and relatively insignificant. All that can be added are some words of description.

In most pictures the Phoenix looks more like an eagle than like any other bird. It has the eagle's curved beak, strong, graceful wings, feathered thighs, well-developed claws, and intelligent eyes. Many drawings also show a crest on the head and a long tail, rather like that of a pheasant. As for its color, the most widely accepted account is that of Pliny, the Roman naturalist. The Phoenix, says Pliny, has a golden head and an azure tail, while the feathers of its body are a mixture of red and purple. The immortal bird must be as beautiful as it is rare.

Over the centuries many people have wondered whether the Phoenix has any connection with the appearance and habits of a real bird. One or two authorities have suggested the bird of paradise, and on the surface this seems like a good suggestion. Birds of paradise, of which there are several species, are among the most spectacularly colored of all birds. Even the name seems right, for where else did the Phoenix live but in paradise? Disappointingly, however, birds of paradise are found only in Australia and New Guinea. Almost certainly, therefore, the birds were unknown to the inhabitants of the Mediterranean, Arabia, and Egypt, the people who made the myth. The first bird-of-paradise plumes were brought

BIRD OF PARADISE

to Europe in 1522, many centuries too late to have influenced the growth of the Phoenix legend. We shall have to look farther, or rather nearer, for a living "ancestor."

Many writers have favored the purple heron of Egypt for the honor of model Phoenix. The principal qualifications of this bird are its reddish-purple color, its crest, and the facts that it often builds its nest in the top of a tall palm tree, was associated with the worship of the sun at On-Heliopolis, and is called in Egyptian the *benu,* which also means palm tree. Furthermore, in Greek, the language in which the Phoenix was first introduced into Europe, the word for palm tree is none other than *phoenix.* If purple heron equals *benu,* which equals palm tree, which equals *phoenix,* it would certainly seem that that part of our problem is solved. Another point in favor of this view is that the bird called the Phoenix in the earliest Egyptian drawings and carvings is long legged, short tailed, and long necked, exactly like a heron. And finally, it is interesting to note that Phoenicia, the ancient land on the eastern shore of the Mediterranean to which the Phoenix gave its name (or vice versa), was famed for the export of a reddish-purple dye so rare and costly that even today we know it as "royal purple" and associate the color with kingship. All in all, it seems as if we should ask, not "How was the colorful eagle-Phoenix of Pliny related to the *benu?*" but "How did the *benu* become transformed into a bird of such different appearance?"

PURPLE HERON
OR BENU

The Phoenix, however, is something more than the purple heron or any of its other possible "ancestors." No known bird lives hundreds of years, not to mention having such a fabulous life history. No, the Phoenix, like the Dragon, is a representative of one of the forces of nature. Its title, Bird of the Sun, is no accident. For the purposes of the people who made the myth, it *was* the sun. Like the sun, it travels from east to west. Like the sun, it may appear to die, but always rises again. If this were not enough, it would only be necessary to remember that the sacred city to whose altar the young bird brings its parent's ashes is On-Heliopolis, whose Greek name means City of the Sun.

Here, we find that not all the pieces fit properly, or not at first. For the sun does not rise and set once every five hundred years, nor every thousand or two hundred fifty, as other versions of the legend state. Where did the Phoenix acquire its long life? If the bird is indeed the sun, its story must represent some genuine cycle in astronomy. What is it, one must ask, that happens to the sun only once in a very long time? Luckily, we can find a clue in the works of Herodotus, a Greek historian of the fifth century B.C. Herodotus' account of the Phoenix differs from others. He gives the Phoenix' life span as fourteen hundred sixty-one years. That is a very curious number, and one or two modern writers have pointed out that it is the same as the number of years in the so-called Sothic sun cycle, as it occurred in the calendar of the

Phoenix, Bird of the Sun

· · · · · · ·

33

ancient Egyptians. To explain this term briefly, the Egyptians counted their months in such a way that each year came out a quarter-day short of what we now know to be the time really required for the earth to travel once around the sun. In other words, their calendar did not contain a leap year as ours does. Thus, over the centuries the Egyptian new year came around earlier and earlier, and the time required for it to fall again on the original day was just fourteen hundred sixty-one years (the number of quarter-days required to make three hundred sixty-five and a quarter days, or one full year).

Now we may guess what was the true meaning of the Phoenix. If Herodotus was right, the Bird of the Sun made its journey back to the place of its birth whenever the calendar came out even. But the figure fourteen hundred sixty-one would mean nothing to the Greeks, the Phoenicians, the Persians, or the other peoples who might have heard the legend, for they did not have the same calendar. It is possible that in telling the story they would remember only that the bird was very long lived. Numbers like five hundred would convey the idea of great age as well as any others, once the tellers of the tale had forgotten the true meaning of the Phoenix and believed it to be a rare and marvelous but real bird.

The Phoenix, like the Dragon, has a Chinese counterpart, called the *feng-huang*. In its pictures it often resembles the Chinese pheasant, perhaps with the addition of a peacock's tail. The Chinese Phoenix is another of the Four Benevolent Creatures, each of which is supreme among its particular kind. Thus the Unicorn (whom we shall meet again in Chapter VI) is the chief of all four-footed beasts, the Tortoise of all shelled beasts, the Dragon of all scaly beasts, and the Phoenix of all birds. Its plumage is said to be a beautiful blend of the five colors, while its voice is a musical harmony of the five notes. It has its origin in the sun, and the other three hundred sixty varieties of birds gather around it wherever it goes. It bathes only in the purest of waters and sleeps each night in a cave. To see the Phoenix is considered very fortunate, as it shows itself only when the Empire is prosperous and justly governed. Similarly, the disappearance of the Phoenix is an omen of misfortune.

Though the origins of the Chinese Phoenix are even more doubtful than those of the western type, it is clear from the description above that like its brother it is a sun symbol (born in the sun, spends the night in a dark place beneath the earth) and has some connection with the calendar (the number three hundred sixty being the number of days in a year of twelve thirty-day months).

The farther we go on our quest for mythical beasts, the more examples we shall find of situations much like this one. We shall find real creatures, like the heron; symbolic beasts, like the Bird of the Sun; difficulties with language like the use of the Greek word *phoenix;* misunderstandings due to differences in cultures, like the problem of the Egyptian calendar; and just plain mysteries. Deliberate lies, exaggerations, and hoaxes will play their part too. One thing is certain: we will never find answers that are true in the same way the answers to mathematical problems are true. We will only find probabilities, and in every case the judgment of what is the real "truth" will be up to the individual.

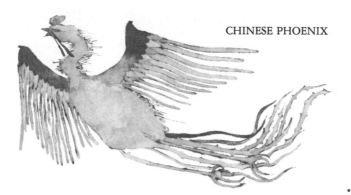

CHINESE PHOENIX

Phoenix, Bird of the Sun

The Basilisk, IV
King Serpent

THE Basilisk is neither the most attractive nor the most impressive looking among imaginary creatures. Yet there are one or two things about it which make it unusual, even in unnatural history.

In the first place, the Basilisk (or, as it was sometimes called, the Cockatrice) was quite small as monsters go. Begin by imagining an ordinary lizard two or three feet long—not a very fearsome sight, even when one adds that the creature had eight legs and the head of a rooster. It might almost be considered an amusing curiosity, like the real but peculiar little

The Basilisk,
King Serpent

• • • • • •

animal known as the duck-billed platypus. Nevertheless, the Basilisk was one of the most widely feared monsters of the Middle Ages, for all writers agreed that merely to catch sight of it was certain death. The victim simply expired on the spot, with no time to give warning to anyone else who might be about. Some authorities stated that feeling its breath, or even hearing it hiss was equally fatal. It is not surprising, therefore, that naturalists before the year 1500 referred to the Basilisk as the King of Serpents, just as the lion was called the King of Beasts. In its portraits the Basilisk often wears a golden crown to show that it is a king.

You may well ask how the creature could be described so fully, if everyone who had seen it was dead. But this was not the kind of question that could be asked during the centuries of which we are speaking. Respect for the opinion of the Authorities (meaning the writers of Greek and Roman times) was too great. It was enough for the scholars that the Basilisk was described by the Roman naturalist Pliny and mentioned by the biblical prophet Isaiah. And, of course, the ordinary people did not consult even the scholars. They *knew* the Basilisk existed, because their grandfathers and their grandfathers' grandfathers had said it did.

There was another factor that bolstered general belief in the Basilisk: the King of Serpents was a very inconspicuous beast. If a Dragon were living in your neighborhood, you would be pretty sure to know it, but a Basilisk might lurk in dark corners, rock crevices, and other out-of-the-way places. This, of course, made it all the more feared, for in contrast to the sportsmanlike rattlesnake it gave no warning of its nearness. Thus, even in the big cities, tales of the Basilisk flourished far into the sixteenth century.

The life history of the Basilisk is strange, even among those of imaginary monsters. Isidore of Seville, a Jewish scholar of the early Middle Ages, wrote that the King of Serpents was born in the days of the Dog Star (that is, in the hot and sickly days of late summer). It was hatched from the egg of a nine-year-old cock—surely a most unnatural start in life, since male birds are not in the habit of laying eggs. The Basilisk's strange origin was so well known that any rooster who was suspected of intending to lay an egg was in danger of its life. In the fifteenth century a law court in the city of Basel held a trial at which the defendant was a cock accused of un-roosterlike activity. The unfortunate bird was found guilty and executed. It is not reported, however, whether a Basilisk did in fact hatch from the egg in question.

In any event, the whole weight of tradition assures us that such eggs *were* laid, and were found to be round as a ball and shell-less. A toad then acted as foster mother, guarding the eggs until they hatched.

There is some disagreement as to where the full-grown Basilisk preferred to live. Many accounts place it in cities, or in the ordinary countryside, but some people insisted that the creature was native to deserts. If this was so, perhaps the desert was made by the Basilisk's own venom, which destroyed everything in the neighborhood including plant life.

There are several tales which indicate that Basilisks were much commoner in early times than they were thought to be later. It is said, for example, that a plague of the little monsters once laid waste the whole of England. The country was only saved by a nameless hero who walked up and down the land in a suit of armor polished mirror-bright. In this way the Basilisks were all killed by the sight of their own reflections. (This was the standard, indeed the only, method of dealing with them.) If we think about it, we will see that the poor man in the mirror suit must have had to keep his eyes closed in order to avoid the deadly sight of his prey. One can imagine his stumbling into trees, falling into rivers, and generally having a miserable time of it. The task must have taken

years to perform. What a shame that the valiant fellow's story is not better known. Surely he deserves as much praise as the heroes who merely passed an idle hour in slaying a Dragon!

Another story about the Basilisk shows it in a great city. The tale was found carved on a stone and gives us perhaps the only authentic street address of a monster. The year was A.D. 1202 and the place was the city of Vienna, at Number Seven, Schönlaterngasse, home of a master baker named Garhibl. Now, at one time Garhibl had had an apprentice lad called Hans, who had been dismissed for having dared to ask for the hand of the baker's lovely daughter Apollonia. The lad had made his plea early one morning, at cockcrow, in fact, and Garhibl had sneeringly replied that Hans might marry Apollonia "when that crowing cock lays an egg." He sent the suitor away in despair, and of course we can guess what happened.

Not long after, Garhibl's housemaid went to fetch water one morning and found that the well gave off a horrible smell. The baker's new apprentice went down to investigate but was overcome by the fumes. Just then there happened to be passing the Master of Justice of Vienna, a learned man named Jacobus. On hearing what had occurred, he announced that the cause of the trouble was undoubtedly a Basilisk. It was well known, he informed the crowd that had now gathered, that the only way to kill the beast was with a mirror. Not surprisingly, however, none of the spectators was anxious to climb down into the slimy well to test Jacobus' statement. Finally, along came Hans, the ex-apprentice, who volunteered to make the descent. Obtaining a mirror and slithering into the well with his eyes shut, he killed the monster in the approved way. And since it was obvious to all that the Basilisk had actually been born from the cock's egg which Garhibl had specified, the baker had no choice but to yield his daughter to the happy hero. The whole tale is a fine example of what may happen to those who speak slightingly of the King of Serpents or any of his imaginary fellows. For if Garhibl had had a proper respect for the power of the monster, he would never have tempted fate by making his rash promise.

This, then, was the Basilisk, a sly and deadly terror. We may be glad, on the whole, that it was only a myth. But was there any real creature on which the story might have been based? One good clue to this question is found in the traditional description of the egg from which the monster is hatched. Round, shell-less white eggs, though never laid by roosters, are quite common among snakes. Another clue is the European tradition that the only animal immune to the Basilisk's poison is the weasel. This belief is also widely held concerning a relative of the weasel, the Indian mongoose. Mongooses do, indeed, kill and eat the deadly Indian cobra and other snakes without apparent harm, although research has shown that the animal is not really safe from the effects of the cobra's poison, but is so agile that it avoids being bitten. Nevertheless, here is a weasel-like creature who was once widely thought to be immune to the deadly bite of a serpent which hatches from a round, shell-less egg. Only one more piece of evidence need be added. There are in Africa several kinds of cobra that can spit their poison at their victims. Their aim is often very accurate at distances of up to several feet, and if they succeed in hitting the eyes, the victim may be temporarily or permanently blinded. So here we have a very strong candidate for the original Basilisk—a snake that can either blind at a distance or kill on contact.

Another possible choice is the scorpion, a poisonous creature that lives in warm climates and has an unpleasant reputation for hiding itself in bureau drawers, empty shoes, and other unexpected places. Although its bite is generally not deadly, it is painful. Probably its reputation as a menace was greatly exaggerated in northern Europe. Being a relative of the spider, it naturally has more legs than do members of the lizard family—eight, in fact. Another notable feature of the scorpion is that it carries its tail (where the sting is found) curled up over its back, in the position in which the Basilisk's tail is most often pictured. We should bear in mind, however, that the artists may have been in the habit of curling the Basilisk's tail for

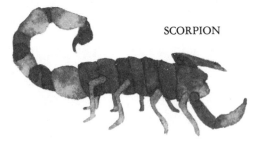

SCORPION

decoration or to save space, and not because it was really thought to carry it that way.

There is just one other thing that must be said in favor of the scorpion as "ancestor" of the King of Serpents. In at least a few of its early portraits the Basilisk is shown with a second head at the end of its curled tail. This would have been a reasonable sort of mistake for anyone who had never seen a scorpion but who might have heard that its "bite" was in its tail. And certainly it is true that the cobra and the scorpion would have been equally unfamiliar and fabulous to the people of northern Europe, who feared the Basilisk so heartily for so long.

Minor Monsters

V

From ghoulies and ghosties
and long-leggety beasties
and things that go bump in the night,
good Lord, deliver us.
                    SCOTTISH SAYING

IN any zoo, real or imaginary, there are some creatures that form the main attraction and some, perhaps
no less interesting, that get less attention. But it
would never do to miss these lesser beasts altogether,
though they may be rare or small or all but unknown.

First, let us glance at two rather remarkable birds
of Arabia. One is probably already familiar from *The
Arabian Nights.* It is, of course, the Roc, whose most
remarkable characteristic is its size. They say that its
flight darkens the sun, and that Sinbad the Sailor, that
legendary adventurer, came upon a Roc's egg and

mistook it for a great white temple dome. The Roc is dangerous as well as awe inspiring. It feeds its young on live elephants and also likes to snack on human beings.

The Roc is also mentioned by Marco Polo, the Italian who traveled to the then nearly unknown land of China in the thirteenth century. According to him the fame of the Roc had spread as far as China, and its ruler, the Great Khan, sent an envoy to the bird's reputed home on the island of Madagascar. The envoy came back with a feather ninety spans long and was given a fine reward for his trouble. Now, taking a span at its traditional value of nine inches, that feather would have been a whopping sixty-eight feet long, and we may be quite certain that no bird of such an outrageous size ever existed. Nevertheless, it does seem as if the people of Madagascar might have had good reason to believe their island was home to some sort of exceptionally large, unknown bird. In the eighteen hundreds, travelers began bringing back from Madagascar fragments of enormous eggs, which the natives sometimes used as water containers. One complete egg measured 12¼ by 9⅜ inches and had a capacity of 2⅓ gallons, making it six times as large as an ostrich egg. But what was the bird that had laid this outsize curiosity? Later scientists discovered on the island the fossil remains of an extremely large species of bird resembling the ostrich but considerably taller, to which they gave the scientific name of *Aepyornis maximus.* Though *Aepyornis* must have become extinct several hundred years ago and certainly never flew at all, being too heavy like its cousin the ostrich, it seems very likely that confused memories of its existence, taken with the still-visible remains of its great eggs, were responsible for the legend of the Roc. Incidentally, the Great Khan's feather, if it ever existed, probably came from one of Madagascar's many tall palm trees, whose fronds, though not ninety spans long, may still be well over ten feet in length and are shaped very much like feathers.

The Roc's neighbor the Safat is famed not for its size, but for its high flying. Virtually nothing is known of the Safat except that the female flies far above the limits of human eyesight. Its eggs are laid while it is in the air, and have so far to fall that they hatch before they reach the ground. If jackals or hyenas eat the fragments of the shell that eventually fall to earth, they will run mad and die.

Far from Arabia, in Argyllshire, Scotland, lives the Boobrie, a monstrous bird that inhabits freshwater lochs, or lakes, and is said to fly up out of the water to prey upon calves and sheep. The creature is black all over and shaped like a long-necked water bird. One man who claimed to have seen it said its bill was seventeen inches long and hooked like an eagle's, while its webbed feet were armed with enormous claws and its cry was like the bellow of an angry bull. In truth, the Boobrie sounds like nothing so much as a giant version of a waterfowl such as the loon or cormorant, both of which are known to submerge completely as they dive after fish and sometimes rise out of the water with a loud and startling commotion.

Turning from birds to creatures of the cold-blooded kind, we find before us the Amphisbaena. Although medieval writers assure us that the Amphisbaena is a reptile, it looks in pictures much more like a kind of long-necked bird, perhaps a goose or cormorant. In most respects it is a fairly unspectacular beast, being neither vicious, poisonous, nor of great

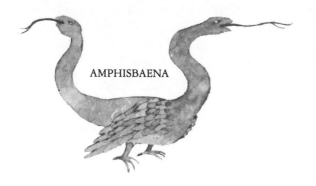

AMPHISBAENA

size. However, it has the distinction of having two heads, the second of which grows on the end of a long, snaky tail. For a finishing touch, both heads often have little round ears like those of a squirrel. Of its habits we know only that it is said to stand the cold better than other reptiles and that when the female hatches her eggs, one head watches while the other sleeps. The Amphisbaena is a shy little monster, and when frightened, it grasps one head with the jaws of the other, thus turning itself into a loop, and rolls rapidly away from its pursuer.

As it happens, there is a real Amphisbaena, although it is far less colorful than the legendary one. The name belongs to a species of limbless lizard that lives underground. Its body is of about the same thickness from head to tail, so that a careless observer might be at a loss to say which was which. Thus, apparently, arose the tale of the two-headed serpent. But why the creature should have been endowed with wings and legs is still unclear.

Another winged reptile is the Wyvern. It is variously described as a small two-legged Dragon and a Basilisk with wings and a Dragon's head. When one comes to think of it, there is little difference between the two. The Wyvern appears frequently in European heraldry, where it is symbolic of plagues and war because it is said to have a poisonous sting. A similar monster called the Skoffin appears in Icelandic legend. In neither case, however, did anyone scoff at these creatures, for both Wyvern and Skoffin were well known in the early Middle Ages and were thought to guard treasure, like their more fearsome cousin the Dragon.

Before leaving the reptile tribe, we must say a brief word about a monster whom the Indians of North America called the Piasa. Almost nothing is known of its habits except what may be deduced from its title, The Bird Which Devours Men. However, there was, before it was destroyed by weather in the last century, a large portrait of the Piasa on a cliff face. There one could see a most remarkable monster who sported horns, red eyes, a beard, a scaly body, feathered wings, and a long, jointed tail. Whether the Piasa can correctly be called a Dragon may never be known, but it is noteworthy in its own right, and one of our authentic native monsters.

Among water dwellers there are three who claim our attention. Two of them, the Hippocampus and the Campchurch, seem to be closely related. The former is a sort of sea horse, having a dolphin's tail in place of its rear legs. With white mane flying it was said to swim at small boats in an attempt to capsize them, a description that sounds suspiciously like that of a large wave with spray blowing from it. The Campchurch, on the other hand, is a sea Unicorn. More precisely, it is of stag size, with a single three-and-a-half-foot horn on its head and webbed feet in place of hoofs in the rear. The Campchurch was thus twice mythical, for the Unicorn on whom it was modeled was also unreal. The Campchurch filled a necessary place in the medieval scheme of things, for scientists of those days believed that every land animal had its equivalent form in the sea. From this belief we get such animal names as sea lion, sea elephant, sea cow, and sea leopard. As recently as 1575, a French traveler named André Thévet reported sighting a Campchurch in the Straits of Malacca, off the coast of the Malay Peninsula. Since the narwhal, which gave its horn to the Unicorn and sounds remarkably like the Campchurch, does not range as far south as these straits, one is inclined to wonder whether Thévet was privileged to see the long, sharp bill of a swordfish spearing through the waves.

Australia is the home of a remarkable beast called the Bunyip. In one rather fanciful description it was said to be the size of a bullock, with the head and neck of an emu (a flightless, ostrichlike bird), the mane and tail of a horse, and the flippers of a seal. It laid eggs and lived mainly on crayfish, although it would also eat people when it could. Such a creature

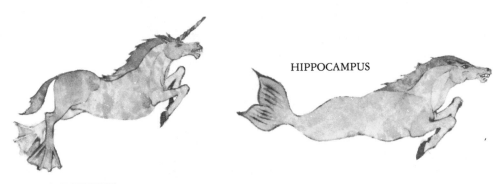

HIPPOCAMPUS

CAMPCHURCH

must sound utterly absurd until we remember that Australia is actually the home of two very genuine egg-laying mammals, the duck-billed platypus and the spiny anteater, and that descriptions of unknown animals inevitably sound unlikely. Consider, for example, what happened to some sailors of the Dutch East India Company who, in the seventeenth century, were among the first to return to Europe from the land later known as Australia. Bernard Heuvelmans, in his delightful book *On the Track of Unknown Animals,* reminds us that those sailors claimed to have seen a man-sized, long-tailed, deer-headed animal that stood on its hind legs like a bird and hopped like a frog. They were answered with polite smiles, giggles, raised eyebrows, and just plain disbelief. Yet today the kangaroo is as well known as the elephant, the giraffe, or the camel.

This is not, of course, to conclude that the Bunyip really exists, but to point out that strange descriptions may apply to very real creatures, especially when they come from a huge and little-known continent like Australia, which certainly has its share of peculiar animal life. The fact is that Bunyips have been reported from a wide variety of places, centering on southeast Australia, and that the reports most often seem to describe a dog-sized animal, with a round, snoutless head and very small or invisible ears, that lives in rivers and swims with "fins" or flippers. Both Mr. Heuvelmans and Gilbert Whitley of the Australian Museum have suggested that the remarkable-sound-

*The Beasts
of Never*

. . . .

50

ing Bunyip may someday turn out to be a water-dwelling beast (a marsupial or pouched mammal, like most other animals of the continent) that resembles a seal or otter. Or, of course, it may be just another version of our age-old human fear that Something is going to rear up out of the water and drag us under.

Land-dwelling animals have always been better described than those that live in the water, and imaginary monsters are no exception. Consider the Yale, a remarkable beast found in European heraldry but dating back to a description by the Roman naturalist Pliny and perhaps earlier. The heraldic Yale combines features of the boar, elephant, horse, stag, and unicorn, with a coat that is "argent bezanty," meaning silvery white with yellow spots. Its most arresting characteristics are its two boarlike tusks and the fact that it has movable horns. What a convenience. The Yale can protect itself against attack from two directions at once.

The probability is that the Yale arose from a mistaken interpretation of pictures of some sort of antelope, probably shown in profile in the style of many early artists, so that one horn pointed forward and the other back. The only alternative in showing a two-horned beast from the side was to give it a single horn, and that technique, as we shall see in the next chapter, may have helped give rise to the legend of the Unicorn. On the other hand, it is reported that the Nandi people of Kenya, Africa, prize above all others cattle with horns pointing in opposite directions and that they have a method of training the horns by means of thongs, much as one may train a young tree or shape the human jaw with braces.

Another beast that may have entered folklore through a misunderstanding is the Behemoth. When the early translators of the Bible were at work on the Book of Job, they came upon the Hebrew word *b'hemoth,* which they put into English as Behemoth since they did not know its meaning. The description in Job (Chapter 40, verses 15–24) certainly makes it clear that the beast in question was one to be reckoned with. (The translation used here is the King James Version, which is over three hundred years old.)

> "Behold now the behemoth, which I made with thee; he eateth grass like an ox. . . . He moveth his tail like a cedar. . . . His bones are as strong pieces of brass, his bones are like bars of iron. . . . Behold, he drinketh up a river, and hasteth not: he trusteth that he can draw up Jordan into his mouth. He taketh it with his eyes: his nose pierceth through snares."

All during the medieval period the Behemoth was taken to be an unknown but huge and powerful animal on the basis of this reference, and somewhere along the way Hebrew commentators came up with the additional notion that the Behemoth was exceed-

WARY YALE

ingly shaggy, even though there is nothing in the biblical passage to suggest that. Then, in the late nineteenth century, when paleontologists (scientists who
study fossils) discovered evidence that much of Europe and North America had once been populated
with an extinct species of elephant known as the
woolly mammoth, which had been hunted and pictured in caves by primitive humans, many people
leapt to the conclusion that the two animals were one
and the same. Even today, circus literature and news-
papers may use *behemoth* as a synonym for *elephant,*
despite the fact that thousands of years separated the
death of the last woolly mammoth from the composi-
tion of the Book of Job. Modern language students,
however, have found a much more plausible source
for the Behemoth in the Egyptian word *p-ehe-mau.*
The word in Egyptian means literally "water ox," but
it probably refers to the hippopotamus. And if you
think that the ancients would not have described the
hippo as an ox, it should be pointed out that our own
English word *hippopotamus* means in Greek "river
horse." There is even an additional clue as to the
Behemoth's identity that lay concealed in the original
language of the Book of Job. The King James Version
translates as part of verse 21 the line, "He [the Behe-
moth] lieth under the shady trees," but in the more
accurate Revised Standard Version, the same line
goes, "Under the lotus plants he lies." Certainly,
the real-life hippopotamus is never more at home
than when up to its fat neck in the River Nile,

*Minor
Monsters*

. . . . . .

53

surrounded by the floating flowers of the lotus plant.

In similar fashion, the name of the sea-dwelling Leviathan, described immediately after the Behemoth in Chapter 41 of Job, has become attached in many people's minds to the whale, although the probability is that it refers to the crocodile. (The Leviathan is more fully described in Chapter VIII.)

It is appropriate, perhaps, that the saying at the beginning of this chapter comes from Scotland, for Scottish folklore seems to harbor an amazing number of "things that go bump in the night."

In addition to the Boobrie, which we have just met, and the Loch Ness Monster, which has Chapter IX all to itself, Scotland has given us a notable water monster and two other creatures that are unclassifiable.

The Kelpie, or water horse (also called the Each Uisge, pronounced *ech ooshkya*) can assume a variety of shapes, but most often appears as a young horse, either a rough, ugly one or a handsome beast that lures the unwary to disaster. Those who mount the Kelpie may find that they cannot get off again because of the animal's sticky skin, and they are usually drowned and devoured when the Kelpie rushes back into the water. In one story seven children were killed in this way, and an eighth was only saved because he became suspicious on noting that the Kelpie's back grew longer to accommodate each additional rider. Like Pegasus, the Kelpie can be tamed by anyone brave enough to bridle it, and the story goes that a Scotsman called Graham of Morphie once bridled a Kelpie and forced it to haul stones for the new castle he was building. When the job was done, Graham loosed his helper. The overworked beast galloped straight into the loch, raising its head from the safety of deep water to cry warningly,

"Sore back and sore bones,
    Driving the Lord of Morphie's stones.
The Lord of Morphie'll never thrive
    So long as the Kelpie is alive!"

Tradition relates that this curse was so effective that the Grahams of Morphie never knew a lucky day from that time on.

Somewhat similar is the Welsh Afanc, a monster like an enormous beaver that was once said to inhabit a whirlpool in the River Conwy, sucking down anyone or anything unlucky enough to fall in.

Another Scottish "beastie" is the unpleasant Brollachan. The name itself means "a shapeless thing" in Gaelic, the old language of the Scots, and shapeless the Brollachan is. They say it has no features at all except eyes and a mouth, and can utter only two words, the Gaelic for *myself* and *yourself*. In addition, it is the child of a Fuath, a dangerous water fairy. In one story a cripple called Ally Murray discovered one night that a Brollachan had crept right up beside him as he sat before his peat fire. When Murray threw more fuel on the fire, some sparks flew out and scorched the Brollachan, which shrieked aloud. In rushed a great, angry Fuath, demanding to know who had hurt her child. "Myself and yourself!" howled the Brollachan. "And isn't that a lucky thing," said the Fuath, "for if it had been anyone else, I'd surely get him for it!" The same idea is found in the ancient Greek tale of Odysseus, in which the hero tells the one-eyed giant Polyphemus that his name is Nobody. Later, after Odysseus has blinded Polyphemus in escaping from his cave, the giant calls on his friends for help; but they are confused when he insists that "Nobody" injured him. Such resemblances are not mere coincidence, for folktales are passed on by word of mouth over vast distances, and a good story may live on in various forms for many hundreds of years.

Much more horrifying than the Brollachan is the Nuckelavee. In fact, of all the monsters in this book, it is the one I would least like to meet on a dark night. At first sight the Nuckelavee looks like a huge man astride an equally huge horse, except that horse and rider are one creature. If you should be foolish enough to linger and look more closely, you would

Minor
Monsters

see that the horse-head has a mouth that gapes from ear to ear and only a single, fiery red eye. Worst of all, the Nuckelavee has no skin, only a mass of raw flesh through which the black blood can be seen running and the white, ropy sinews stretching as it moves. The monster comes up out of the sea and spreads terror, blight, and death wherever it goes. The only escape from it is to cross running water. Like many monsters whose origins go back to pagan times, the Nuckelavee is believed to fear fresh water because it symbolizes the water of Christian baptism.

Now, having met several perfectly genuine monsters, we should perhaps say a word about one nonmonster. The salamander has been listed in so many works on fabulous beasts that it is almost disappointing to have to banish it to the realm of reality. Ancient manuscripts picture the salamander as a small, smooth-skinned, lizardlike creature, supposed to inhabit swamps and other damp places. It liked water so much that it was believed to be immune to the effects of fire. Indeed, later legends said that the salamander actually went looking for blazing hearths in order to bask in the flames.

For this reason powdered salamander was much used in medieval medicine as a remedy for fevers, burns, and even hot tempers. The theory was that patients, by taking salamander, would be protected from those influences of the stars that were causing the element of heat to have too much power over them. That, of course, was pure balderdash. Yet, curiously enough, the tale of the salamander in the flame was not. The salamander is a real and even common little amphibian that lives most of its life in or near water and looks much as described above. However, adult specimens do travel about on land, and where winters are cold they often hibernate in some such place as a hollow log. Over centuries of wood-gathering in Europe, it must sometimes have happened that a log containing a sleeping salamander was thrown on the fire. Happily, the victims were not always consumed. For the salamander, when frightened (as who would not be, waking up with the house afire?), exudes a milky fluid that generally acts as a repellent toward hungry larger animals. In a few cases, though, this fluid may have helped shield the salamander from the heat long enough for it to make its escape from the flames, much to the amazement of those who saw. Thus, it is more through tradition than by virtue of the facts that the salamander finds a place in the ranks of mythical monsters.

Not all the creatures in this book have ancient ancestries, and neither are they all as frightening as the Dragon or as impressive as the Griffin. The unnatural history of North America has given us an assortment of critters that inspire more chuckles than shivers and serve to remind us that those who have no venerable traditions are quite capable of making some up. Most of the animals described below are featured in "tenderfoot stories," that is, tall tales told (even today) to impress strangers with the bizarre wildlife of a particular region.

In the American Southwest and northern Mexico, they talk about the famous Cactus Cat, a feline with thorny fur, spiny ears, a branched tail, and sharp blades of bone above its forefeet. At night the Cactus Cat likes to slash at the bases of giant cactus trees with its knifelike forearms. The cactus sap flows out and ferments into mescal, a very potent drink that the Cats love. They soon become so howling, yowling drunk that they go parading around in the moonlight, rasping their bony forearms together and rousing the desert for miles around with their infernal racket.

Not to be confused with the Cactus Cat is the Splinter Cat, found from the Great Lakes to the Gulf of Mexico. This cat has a hard, bony head and feeds exclusively on raccoons and wild honey, both of which are to be found in the hollows of trees. The Cat's method of hunting is to spring at one tree after another and shatter them to splinters with its bony head until it finds what it is looking for. The damaged

Minor Monsters

· · · · · ·

57

forests it leaves in its wake are often mistakenly blamed on tornadoes and hurricanes. A subspecies of this cat, called the Sliver Cat, achieves the same effect with a ball-shaped knob on the end of its tail. Its eye holes are vertical rather than horizontal, and it has red eyes.

The lumberjacks who worked with the legendary Paul Bunyan in the Great North Woods knew the Sliver Cat, and many more remarkable animals, of which only two can be mentioned here. The Goofus Bird is found near the Big Onion River in Minnesota and is identified by its habit of building its nest upside down and flying backward. Folks say of it, "The critter doesn't give a darn where it's going, it just wants to see where it's been." Perhaps there is some strange influence in the air or water of the region, for it is also home to a fish called the Goofang, which always swims backward to keep the water out of its eyes. People who have seen it say it is "about the size of a sunfish, only larger."

California's high chaparral country is inhabited by the famous Tripodero, a creature with a long, tube-like snout, a tail resembling a kangaroo's, and two legs that can be shortened or lengthened like telescopes. When searching for prey, the Tripodero raises itself above the dense brush by expanding its legs. Anything it sees, it kills by shooting a hard pellet of sun-dried clay from its snout, as if from a pea-shooter. It then contracts its legs and wriggles its compact body between the stems to get to its meal.

Finally, there is the fierce and unpredictable Gwinter, which some say got its name from the fact that "Ya never know what it's gwinter do." It is a horned grazing animal that lives on mountain slopes in Texas. Because of its habitat, the legs on one side of its body are longer than those on the other side. This is convenient for grazing but presents a problem, in that the Gwinter must always head in the same direction because it will fall over if it turns so its short legs are on the downhill side. For this reason, there are "left-handed" and "right-handed" Gwinters. The animals are very short-tempered, and in former times mighty battles ensued whenever two Gwinters met head to head. Eventually, all the animals on the weaker side got killed, and each mountain now has only one type of Gwinter. They will attack human beings as readily as each other, but efforts to eliminate them have failed. That is because, when pursued, they run in uphill spirals until, at the mountain peak, they turn inside out and escape in the opposite direction. The Gwinter is therefore nearly as uncatchable as the Unicorn, which we are about to meet in the next chapter. No self-respecting Texan would admit that the Gwinter might be equipped with a mere single horn, however.

The Untamable VI
Unicorn

"Well, now that we **have** *seen each other,"*
said the Unicorn, "if you'll believe in me,
I'll believe in you. Is that a bargain?"
LEWIS CARROLL

IN the midnight forest the dark oak trees are still
under the stars. The pale wildflowers in the clearing
have furled their petals for the night. Suddenly it appears, a milk-white creature with the proud form of a
horse. You may not notice its cloven hoofs or curling
beard, but you see the curved neck, the silver mane,
the graceful tail. Then it moves its head, and the
moonlight runs like seawater along the pearly spiral
of its horn. There is no sound, but at the next heart-
beat the clearing is once again empty of all but the
night.

You have seen the Unicorn, as it might have ap-

The Untamable
Unicorn

peared in a tale of fifteenth-century France. It was the most beautiful, the most noble, the most elusive of legendary creatures. It walked alone; it was gentle and proud, but would fight to the death if attacked. The unicorn could be killed but not captured, and unlike Pegasus it would never be tamed by a human master with a golden bridle. Yet the Unicorn of the later Middle Ages had once been a very different animal. Its history is more tangled, its origins more diverse, and its roots almost as ancient as those of the Dragon.

The first account of the Unicorn was given by Ctesias, a Greek historian who wrote in the fourth century B.C. Ctesias was visiting the court of the King of Persia, and he kept a journal describing the strange things he had seen or heard of. He wrote, "There are in India certain wild asses which are as large as horses or larger. Their bodies are white, their heads dark red, and their eyes dark blue. They have a horn on the forehead which is about a foot and a half in length. . . . The base of this horn, for some two hands' breadth above the brow, is pure white; the upper part is sharp and of a vivid crimson; and the remainder, or middle portion, is black. . . . The animal is exceedingly swift and powerful, so that no creature, neither horse nor any other, can overtake it."

Ctesias' account was later taken up by Pliny, the Roman naturalist in whose works scholars were to believe unquestioningly for a thousand years. Pliny described an animal with "a stag's head, an elephant's feet, and a boar's tail." He added, "The rest of the body is like that of a horse. It makes a deep lowing noise and one black horn two cubits [about three feet] long projects from the middle of the forehead. This animal, they say, cannot be taken alive." It seems hardly possible that this elephant-footed and brightly colored monstrosity can have had anything to do with the graceful, pure white Unicorn, but in fact it appears to be one of the four principal "ancestors" of the Unicorn as we know it. One might say that the beast intended by these early classical writers was the Unicorn's three-times-great-grandparent.

To discover the origin of the Unicorn of Ctesias and Pliny can be quite upsetting to those who are devoted to the romantic creature of later times. For it is pretty well agreed nowadays that the animal both writers had based their accounts on was—the rhinoceros. A smellier, clumsier, more disagreeable creature would be hard to imagine, but the rhinoceros does have two characteristics that make it a most fitting "ancestor" for the Unicorn. First, it is the only land-dwelling mammal that normally has a single "horn" anywhere near the middle of its head. It is true that a biologist would tell us that the rhinoceros' horn is not really a horn but a collection of tough, hairlike fibers. Nevertheless, horn is what it looks like, and feels like, and certainly it grows singly in the middle of the face, at least in the great Indian rhino, although other species sport two horns.

The next notable thing about the rhino is that when angered it is exceedingly unmanageable, bad tempered, and difficult to capture. It is armored like a tank, may weigh over a ton, and carries a very effective weapon on its nose, just where it can most easily be stuck into someone else. It is no wonder that the Unicorn acquired through the rhinoceros a reputation for being untamable.

The second major source of the Unicorn legend is found in many translations of the Bible, particularly the Book of Job in the sections just before those dealing with the Behemoth and Leviathan, as described in Chapter V. In one passage (Chapter 39, Verses 9–12 of the King James Version), the Lord demands of Job, "Will the unicorn be willing to serve thee, or abide by thy crib? Canst thou bind the unicorn with his band in the furrow? or will he harrow the valleys after thee? Wilt thou trust him, because his strength is great?" The answer to all these questions is plainly no, for the deeds listed are beyond the power of any

The Untamable Unicorn

· · · · · · ·

63

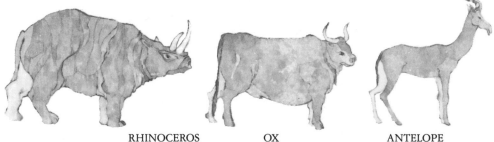

RHINOCEROS   OX   ANTELOPE

individual. The later importance of this passage for the history of the Unicorn was very great, for after the fall of the Roman Empire there followed a thousand years of European history during which it was considered a sin to doubt the literal truth of anything that was written in the Bible. Since the Unicorn was very clearly mentioned there, its existence was as firmly believed in as that of the dog. It was not until a few centuries ago that scholars began to go back and read the original text of Job, which had, of course, first been written in Hebrew. When they did go back, they discovered a strange thing: the Hebrew word *re'em,* which was used in the Book of Job, did not mean Unicorn at all. In fact, it is not certain to this day just what it *did* mean, though it may have been the wild ox. The seventy-two early scholars who translated the Bible into Greek must have cast about in their minds for an animal like the one described, and come up with Ctesias' untamable rhinoceros-Unicorn. In a way, they probably did as well as could be expected, for it would certainly be difficult to think of an animal which would be harder to harness to a plow as the Bible demanded.

In the fourth century A.D., tales of the Unicorn became increasingly common. One of the earliest bestiaries, or books of beast fables, was entitled in Latin *Physiologus* (meaning "The Naturalist") and describes a fierce animal the size of a kid. Other sources give it features that remind us of the antelope, the horse, the ox, or the deer. From this time on, the Unicorn usu-

The Beasts
of Never

· · · · · · ·

64

HORSE   DEER   GOAT

ally wears a goat's beard in honor of the goat it was supposed to resemble.

It is about this period, too, that one first runs across the story of the Unicorn Hunt. The Unicorn was generally believed to be impossible to capture, as we have said, *except* in the following way: A lovely maiden must go and seat herself at the foot of a tree, deep in the forest. Attracted by her beauty and goodness, the Unicorn will then come meekly to her and lay its head in her lap, after which the hunters may come out of hiding and surround it with their spears. In some versions of the tale the noble captive is then led off as a present for the king, but usually the hunters slaughter it brutally, for no apparent reason except the joy of killing or for the sake of its valuable horn.

This story was immensely popular in the Middle Ages, and those who told it often gave it a moral. Either the Unicorn was made to represent the virtue of meekness, or else it symbolized the sacrifice of Christ.

It is rather pleasant to learn that this tale of treachery seems to be derived from an extremely old myth about the sun and moon which did not have the same tragic ending. According to Odell Shepard in his *The Lore of the Unicorn,* the tale was based on an ancient Babylonian tradition that described a battle between a lion and a one-horned animal resembling the wild ox. Seals made of baked clay or carved in gems, some of them several thousand years old, show a lion at-

The Untamable Unicorn

tacking or chasing this Unicorn-like beast. From other elements in the mythology of the time, it becomes clear that the characters represent heavenly bodies. The golden lion is the sun, and the Unicorn is the moon because the single horn resembles its crescent. The complete story relates how the Unicorn chases the lion across the sky until the lion dodges behind the tree that grows at the root of the world. Then the Unicorn, charging straight ahead, pierces the tree with its horn and is held fast so that the lion can come out and devour it. But nothing is permanent in the cycles of astronomy; the new moon always follows the old. And so in the legend the Unicorn always returns with renewed life to chase the sun-lion again across the sky. This tradition of hostility between the two animals lingered on long after the sun-moon myth had been changed into that of the Unicorn and the Maiden. Perhaps one evidence of this is the old nursery rhyme that says:

> The Lion and the Unicorn
>   Fighting for the Crown
> The Lion beat the Unicorn
>   All about the Town.

Of course, the rhyme was intended to refer to the well-known disagreements of the Lion of England with the Unicorn of Scotland, but the fact that the two warring nations chose those particular beasts to represent them in heraldry is not entirely an accident.

By the beginning of the Middle Ages the Unicorn in the tale of the Hunt had made a secure place for itself in European folklore. No one doubted its existence, any more than you would disbelieve in the great blue whale, although you have probably never seen a live one. It was at this time that the Unicorn began to become the noble and graceful creature we met at the beginning of this chapter. The engravings and carvings of the time most often show it in its horselike form. Perhaps this was a result of its reputation for speed, although from the sources available it might just as easily have taken shape as a goat, ass, or ox. And once it had acquired a definite shape, so to speak, legend began to give it a definite character.

First, as we already know, it was impossible to capture alive. Second, it never appeared in herds, like most beasts of the horse and cattle kind, but always preferred to remain solitary. This was probably another characteristic which it owed to Ctesias, for the rhinoceros also seems to shun its own kind. In fact, some writers went so far as to state that there existed only one Unicorn at a time, so that, like the Phoenix, it never had any family life. Now, it is all very well to be beautiful and solitary, but one cannot help feeling that it would be sad for the Unicorn to have to live out an entire lifetime alone. Happily, therefore, there is at least one story that tells something about the way Unicorns lived in the wild.

Once, they say, King Arthur set sail from England to visit Brittany on the coast of France. But the ship's captain was not familiar with the route and had the ill luck to run the vessel aground on an unknown island. All efforts to move the ship having failed, King Arthur took himself off for a walk through a nearby wood to try to find a way out of the predicament, and as he walked, he met a dwarf. "God save Your Majesty," said the dwarf, bowing low, "how can I serve you?" Arthur explained his difficulty, but the dwarf made light of it. "That is easily remedied," he said. "My son is away hunting at the moment, but when he returns he will be honored to move your ship for you."

Considering the small size of his companion, Arthur was not very hopeful that anything would come of his promise, but he was much too courteous to say so. Having nothing better to do, therefore, he decided to sit down and wait for the dwarf's son. "Your Majesty," said the dwarf, "I will tell you the story of my life to pass the time, if you will be so gracious as to listen."

Many years ago, the dwarf related, he had been shipwrecked on this lonely island with his infant son. As soon as might be, he set about building a shelter for them, for he had no idea how long they might be stranded there. While he was at work, it was his plan to leave the baby safe in a hollow tree. Therein he found two little brown fawnlike creatures, but thinking they would keep the child warm, he left him as intended and went to work nearby. Before long, the mother of the two little creatures returned, and she was not a deer but a great white Unicorn. The dwarf was terrified for his son and would have thrown away his life in attacking the Unicorn, but that he saw how gently she treated the baby. In fact, she seemed to accept him as her own and allowed him to nurse with the two young Unicorns. From that day on the father was astonished to see how the baby thrived. In the midst of his telling Arthur what a fine boy his son had become, they heard a crashing in the woods. "Why, here comes my son now!" exclaimed the dwarf as a great brawny giant strode into the clearing. Indeed, the dwarf had been right—Unicorn's milk had done wonders for the little fellow, who was well over thirty feet tall. After that, of course, it was only a short time until the obliging giant had refloated the ship and been thanked by the King, who continued his journey, wiser in the ways of Unicorns than most authorities have been since.

There is still one other characteristic of the Unicorn that made it important in medieval Europe, and that is the power of its horn. First, the horn was of

great value to its owner. The Unicorn was supposed
to be able to save itself from capture by leaping head-
first over cliffs. It would then land on the point of its
horn, which acted as a sort of shock absorber and
bounced it gently back to its feet, much to the amazement of the watchers atop the cliff. It may be that this
legendary ability more properly belongs to the Al-
pine ibex, which is justly famed for its sureness of
foot and cliffside escapes. The Unicorn, which had
borrowed so much from so many other beasts, does
not seem to have been shy about adopting the trick
for itself.

In addition, the Unicorn's horn was believed to be
of benefit to others. From earliest times physicians
and scholars had agreed that powdered Unicorn horn
would cure practically every disease, from a cold in
the head to the black plague. It could also purify water. One popular tale about the Unicorn was that it
would dip its horn into springs that had been
poisoned by toads, snakes, or Basilisks, thus making
them safe for other animals to drink from. In gratitude for this service other creatures were supposed to
act as sentinels to warn the Unicorn of the approach
of hunters.

Finally, the value of the horn was brought even
higher because it was thought to be a sure protection
against or cure for poison. Since this was a period
when the nobility looked upon poisoning as just another convenient method of getting rid of an enemy
(a little less messy than stabbing), one can imagine
that kings and dukes would pay almost any price for

*The Untamable
Unicorn*

such protection. In museums one may still see the costly gold and jeweled cups that were made with "Unicorn" horn. The thought behind these utensils was that they would give warning of the presence of poison by sweating or smoking. It is not surprising, therefore, that fragments of the horn were sold for ten times their weight in gold. An entire horn, it was said, would be worth a city.

We may ask now just what it was that buyers received when they paid out their money for Unicorn horn. The answer seems to be—just about anything. Fossil bones, ibex horn, elephant ivory, walrus tusks, and the "horn" of the rhinoceros were all sold by unscrupulous or ill-informed merchants at vast profits.

But there was one kind of Unicorn horn that was so mysterious that it became a part of the legend itself. This was the so-called horn, actually the *tooth,* of the narwhal, a member of the whale family that lives in the cold waters of the Arctic. The male narwhal grows a long, spirally twisted, white tooth out of the upper side of its left jaw. Just why this tooth grows in this manner, no one knows. It does not seem to serve any purpose for its owner, neither for getting food, nor for defense, nor for attracting the female narwhal. But if the narwhal did not have much use for its tooth, the Unicorn did. On those rare occasions when narwhal ivory was washed up on a beach or otherwise came into human hands, it was almost always taken to be the horn of the Unicorn. It seemed made for a fabulous creature of song and legend. And so the Unicorn acquired its proudest ornament.

NARWHAL

Interestingly, rhinoceros "horn," like other, true horns, contains a substance called keratin, which will effervesce, or bubble, in the presence of some types of alkaloid poisons. Knowledge of this fact may once have been at the root of beliefs about Unicorn horn, but it must have passed out of memory before the Unicorn acquired its lovely spiral weapon. For narwhal ivory is tooth, not horn, and contains no keratin.

Once people had come to believe that the narwhal tooth belonged to the Unicorn, it may have influenced the artists and naturalists whose job it was to describe the body that went with the horn. Such a graceful, tapered spiral could hardly be thought to belong to a goatlike or oxlike beast, as many of the old manuscripts suggested.

Thus, finally, we have the elegant and noble Unicorn of the French tapestries. It had the body of a horse, the hoofs of a deer, the beard of a goat, the horn of a sea beast, the ferocity of the rhinoceros, the virtues of a chivalrous knight, and the powers of the magical moon. No other animal before or since has matched it for beauty and dignity.

We have managed to account fairly well for the Unicorn's appearance. But what of its story? Who is the maiden, that the Unicorn should love her? Where is that enchanted forest that sets the scene for this drama of devotion and betrayal? In order even to begin to answer those questions, we must take a long jump back in time and an even longer one into the delightful but perilous realm of speculation.

Consider the tale, related above, of the eternal contest between the golden-maned sun lion, the crescent-horned moon bull, and the "tree at the root of the world." Perhaps the tree is that famous tree at the world's axis (call it Yggdrasil, call it the Tree of Eden) around which, in the ancient mythologies of the West, all cosmic events revolve. In any case, the bull is often identified with the moon and the moon is widely represented as a maiden. It may not be stretching the facts unduly to suppose a connection between the moon's creature and the goddess herself. We might even venture to name two of her many names: she is Artemis or Diana, virgin, huntress, protector of all wild things, and there are many examples from ancient art in which moon, maiden, tree, and horned creature appear together. It may be proper, therefore, that our Unicorn is so often shown with the beasts of field and forest. Unknowingly, the medieval artisans may have been recreating a scene far older than Christian Europe, in which the Maiden and her creatures enjoy a moment of peace and harmony at the foot of the Tree of Life before the cycle turns once again, the lion springs from its hiding place, and the never-ending combat continues.

Was it so, or is it fantasy? We do not know, and perhaps it is only fitting that the Unicorn should keep its mystery and its wildness, never to be imprisoned in a thesis or bound into volumes of logic. It was a great loss to the world of imagination when the Unicorn died, sometime late in the nineteenth century.

For die it did, though much later than many of its mythical fellows. The reason was that for a very long time perfectly honest and sincere people kept reporting having seen the Unicorn in some out-of-the-way place. Missionaries to Canada, travelers in the Far East, explorers in Africa, swore to its existence right up to the time of the first railways.

At this point we must pause and make one thing clear. There really *wasn't* any Unicorn. In spite of all the reports, people who study anatomy and zoology have proved that no animal with cloven hoofs could ever have a single natural horn in the middle of its forehead because of the way the bones must grow together while the animal is still unborn. There is only one kind of tissue from which horn can develop, and it would be impossible for such tissue to form a single true horn in the middle of the forehead. Even the rhinoceros, which does not have cloven hoofs, does not have a true horn.

But if this is so, what were all those seemingly trustworthy travelers seeing that appeared to them so like a genuine Unicorn? No one really knows the answer, but here, in no particular order, are a few of the suggestions that have been made.

First, some may have seen animals that had lost one of their two original horns in a fight or an accident.

Second, some may have seen an animal such as the wild oryx of Africa standing in perfect profile. If one looks at a table from this point of view, it will appear to have only two legs because the other two are hidden, and likewise two long straight horns on an oryx will appear to be only one if looked at straight from the side.

Third, it seems that there are wandering tribes of cattle herders in Africa and elsewhere who have learned the secret of transplanting the horn buds of young cattle so that a single central horn results. This process has been experimentally repeated by a Dr. Dove, an American researcher who successfully produced a one-horned bull. Disappointingly, the bull did not turn into a Unicorn, but remained an ordinary bull in all other respects. Animals such as this are considered the natural leaders among the herders, and it is possible that some of them are referred to in certain of the Unicorn reports.

The Unicorn is still very much a part of our folklore and is of great interest to the public, as may be seen from the following.

In recent years, the Ringling Brothers and Barnum and Bailey Circus featured a creature billed as "The Living Unicorn." The animals (there were actually more than one, as with other famous stars such as "Lassie") were handsome pure white goats whose natural horns had been removed and replaced with single bull's horns, surgically implanted in the middle of their foreheads.

The circus Unicorns were not seriously intended to deceive anyone about the existence of Unicorns. Not so with the report made in 1983 by two men who

The Untamable Unicorn

73

said that while hiking in the Shenandoah National Park, not far from Washington, D.C., they had spotted a horselike white animal with a spiral white horn in the center of its forehead. They had photographs to prove it, but the animal shown would certainly have disappointed any true Unicorn lover. In the words of the *Washington Post* newspaper story, the beast was "a mangy version of a unicorn whose mane resembled a discount-store wig." The two men later admitted they had equipped a rather decrepit horse with the horn (plus gold mane and tail) for a hoax. It seems a shame they couldn't have found a more heroic-looking horse for the role.

Considering the ongoing popularity of the Unicorn legend, it is not surprising that one of the creature's relatives does "survive" in the Orient.

As recently as the first half of this century, the peasants of China still believed in a one-horned animal called the Ch'i-Lin. (The Japanese version is Kirin.) It had a stag's body, a horse's hoofs, an ox's tail, a twelve-foot horn with a fleshy growth on the end, and a voice like the ringing of bronze bells. Its back was multicolored and its belly was yellow. It was of the highest moral character, refusing to eat or harm any living thing, and it could not be captured.

If this word picture makes the Ch'i-Lin sound very much like our Unicorn, actual drawings do not show the same similarity. Perhaps artists have stylized the Ch'i-Lin over the centuries, for its pictures show a rather chunky animal with a relatively short horn and a grinning mouth trimmed with whiskers. Yet the powers of the Ch'i-Lin are, if anything, more impressive than those of its western cousin. Like the Phoenix, the Ch'i-Lin is the bringer of good tidings, an exceedingly lucky sight. Mothers who step in its footsteps have children who grow up to be emperors, philosophers, or saviors of their people. The appearance of the Ch'i-Lin is a sign that all is well with the kingdom of China and that the ruler is just and virtuous.

Although there is no general agreement on the subject, most scholars tend to support the theory that the Ch'i-Lin is not native to China, but was imported —a product, perhaps, of some of the same traditions that gave birth to the Unicorn of the West. Thus, although the first Ch'i-Lin is supposed to have appeared in China at a very early date, during the reign of the semimythical Yellow Emperor, it is very interesting that in the fifteenth century, when Chinese sailors began to make their first regular voyages to the eastern coast of Africa, one of the greatest prizes to be brought back to the imperial court was a live giraffe—an animal that the Chinese immediately identified with the Ch'i-Lin. In fact, the giraffe does have some characteristics that resemble those of the Ch'i-Lin surprisingly closely. Like the Ch'i-Lin it is of a peaceable disposition and eats no flesh. Its back is spotted with several colors of brown and its belly is yellowish. Its tail is tufted like that of the ox and, most strikingly, its horns (though there are two and not one) end in knobs or tufts of hair, a highly unusual feature not found on any other animal. Perhaps strangest of all is the fact that in the Somali language, which is spoken over a good part of the east coast of Africa, the word for giraffe is *girin,* and Chinese scholars note that the spelling "ch'i-lin" is about as close as the Chinese language can come to pronouncing the Somali word. This does not tell us, of course, whether the beast and the word had originally been borrowed from Africa. After all, the home of the Indian one-horned rhino is a great deal closer to China than Africa is, and the Chinese were just that much more likely to have heard of the rhino in the same way Ctesias did.

Nevertheless, it is intriguing to note that wherever it traveled, the Unicorn kept the noble nature that makes it unique among characters human or animal, real or imaginary.

The Untamable
Unicorn

• • • • • •

75

Winged V I I
Wonders

In the swift Rank of these
fell rovers, flies
The **Indian Griffin** *with the*
glistring eyes.
SYLVESTER'S *DU BARTAS*

G R I F F I N S are fearsome and majestic beasts who come of a very ancient family. "They have the shape of an eagle before, and behind the shape of a lion. . . . The griffin is more and stronger than eight lions of these countries and greater and stalworther than a hundred eagles." That is the description given by Sir John de Mandeville, an English traveler of the twelfth century who claimed to have seen these mythical creatures in their native country.

In actual fact, the talkative Sir John may have been

a little bit mythical himself. Certainly there is evidence that he was not who he said he was and that he had not been where he said he had been. He was a fine storyteller, but not a very accurate observer. Nevertheless, his travel book was widely read and accepted in medieval Europe. It confirmed many of the tales of the Griffin that the Crusaders had brought back from the Near East. Soon the fierce eagle-lion became a favorite subject for sculpture and heraldry.

In his celebrated description de Mandeville had omitted one important feature of the Griffin's appearance. The creature's pictures make it clear that it possessed ears, something no eagle ever had. They were long, pointed ears, rather like those of a horse. Just where or how the Griffin got them is a mystery. However, in heraldry they do serve to differentiate the Griffin from the eagle when just the head is shown.

The early Griffins seem to have been a fierce and uncivilized race. They lived, according to Arab and Persian legend, in the mountains of Scythia or western Persia. Their mission was to guard the gold mines of the gods against greedy human beings. Their particular enemies were a tribe called the Arimaspians. These people were quite fearsome themselves, being one eyed and very warlike, yet they generally got the worst of it from the Griffins, who would swoop down on any intruders and carry them away to their golden nests as food for their young. In the same way a mounted man or even a full team of oxen might fall victim to the Griffin's hunger.

This habit of flying off with things was put to good use by sailors of the area, it is said. In times of emergency, as when a boat sprang a leak or was threatened by rocks, the sailors would dress up in animal skins and stand about on deck. Then the Griffins, hovering always in the upper air watching for possible prey, would dive down, snatch up the men, and carry them away to land. But the story does not tell how the men managed to escape from their rescuers. It certainly sounds as if they might have found themselves worse off than before.

Oddly enough, in view of the Griffins' fierceness, there was one way in which they were of benefit to humanity. Their claws were thought to be wonderfully effective medicine for just about any disease. Although not quite as valuable as Unicorn horn, Griffins' claws were much sought after and were often made into drinking cups because liquids drunk from such cups were safe from poison. The ones that are still preserved in museums usually turn out to have come from the heads of ibex or buffalo—sharp, curved horns over a foot long. A creature with claws like these was surely worthy of respect.

If one wished to obtain a Griffin's claw, there was only one reliable method. A holy man must travel through the wilderness until he came upon a Griffin who was ill or hurt. He could then cure the monster by the virtue of his prayers and the grateful patient would reward the saint with a claw, so that suffering human beings might likewise be cured.

As the centuries went by, the nature of the Griffins seems to have changed. As our barbaric ancestors became more civilized, so did their ideas about Griffins. In Italy, at least, the eagle-lions acquired the power of speech and set up an entire Griffin kingdom underground.

There is an Italian tale about a king and queen who were stricken with blindness. They had ruled long and well and were much loved by their people. Hearing of their plight, and out of gratitude for their past kindness, a poor old woman came one day to seek audience with the king and queen. There was a cure for their affliction, she told them, if anyone was bold enough to bring it. Three red feathers from the breast of the Griffin King would surely restore their sight.

Eagerly, the good rulers' three sons agreed to go in search of the precious feathers. Far over land and sea they traveled until they came to an immensely deep well which the old dame had described to them. At its bottom, they had been told, the Griffin King kept his court. But when it came to the test, the two older princes were afraid to go down so far. Only the third brother dared the descent. Down into the fearsome darkness he went, and found himself at last in a great hall full of gold. There, indeed, was the Griffin King, rearing his great bulk, black against the light of underground fires. The Griffin asked what it was the bold young stranger sought. The prince, not at all afraid, was impressed with the Griffin's lordly manner and offered to serve as one of his knights for a year, a month, and a day.

For a long, weary time his brothers waited for him in the sunny world above, fearing him dead. But at last the prince's term was ended, and he claimed the three red feathers as his fee of service. Graciously, the Griffin King granted the request, and the young man returned rejoicing to the upper lands.

This is all we are told about the underground kingdom, though it would be interesting to learn more about the Griffins. For instance, what language was spoken? Did the Griffin knights ever venture aboveground? Whose treasure were they guarding? Nevertheless, the tale is quite informative. It tells us that the Italian Griffins had absorbed the customs of their native land and had set up a feudal kingdom, ruled by a king who based his power on an army of knights and honored his word without treachery. Like the Dragons of China they had developed a social system that mirrored that of the human society around them.

The legend makers were not being misled by reports of a real beast. They created the eagle-lion wholly in their minds, and undoubtedly it had for them some symbolic significance. Just what that significance was, we will have a hard time guessing, however, until we know more of the Griffin. As mentioned above, Persian legend says the Griffins made their home in Scythia, the general region north of the

Black Sea, and certainly Griffins are prominent in Scythian art, where they are most often seen attacking deer or horses. Since the Scythians were nomads who lived by and for their horse herds, we might suppose that the Griffin represented a joining of two dangerous beasts of prey—the eagle that swooped upon the weak and the newborn, and the various great cats that preyed on adult horses when they could.

The Griffins' golden hoards are easily explained also, as the Scythians were famed throughout the ancient world for their wealth in gold dust and the magnificent gold jewelry and utensils they made from it. That indeed may be part of the explanation, but it cannot be all, for if we look once more at the carved seals of the Near East, we find examples of creatures very like Griffins (that is, eagle-headed lions without ears) locked in combat with the god Marduk or his counterpart Bel. In fact, in these images the Griffin is playing the role of one of Tiamat's helpers in the great struggle between Chaos and the gods (see Chapter I). The Griffin in these cases seems hardly different from a Dragon, and if we travel even farther back into mythology, we find an Egyptian Griffin as one of the animals belonging to Seth, a god of storm cloud and whirlwind who later became the embodiment of evil, rather like Satan. Is it only a teasing coincidence that Seth is primarily identified with the wild ass and is known in his human form by the fact that he wears ass's ears, long and pointed, exactly like the Scythian Griffin's? We do not know, and we may never know unless archaeology should uncover for us some bridge to span the gap of miles and years between Egyptian Seth and the fierce predator of the Scythian horse herds.

Later Persian legends speak of a creature not unlike the Griffin in looks but very different in temperament. The Simurg or Senmurv is often described as a dog-bird, although in most of its pictures it is simply a fanciful bird with a long, ornate tail. "Its wings are

like a wide cloud and full of water crowning the mountains," as an ancient manuscript puts it. The Simurg is an agent of the goodwill of the gods and preys upon harmful snakes. Most important, it nests in the Tree of Life. Each time it alights on its branches, it scatters over the world the seeds that cure all evil. There is a Persian story from before the eleventh century that shows some of the similarities of the Simurg to the Griffin.

In those days, the sages say, there was a king's son named Zal who was taken into the wilderness and left to die. The reason was that the poor child had been born with white hair, which was an evil omen. However, as often happens in folk tales, the outcast was rescued by a wild beast, in this case the Simurg. The Dog Bird grew very fond of the boy, who was both brave and clever, and taught him much of his ancient wisdom. Then one night the king, Zal's father, had a dream which told him that his son was alive and should be brought back to the palace to live. The king was overjoyed, for he had been gnawed with remorse since the boy's supposed death. The Simurg heard the king's prayer for the safe return of his son and sadly realized that it was time to send him back to his own people. As a parting gift the great creature gave its foster son one of its own feathers, with instructions to burn it if he was ever in deep trouble. Then the prince returned to his father's court, where he married a beautiful princess and ruled long years

HIPPOGRIFF,
STEED OF MAGICIANS

with honor and wisdom. One day, however, his beloved wife fell gravely ill. Then Zal remembered the
magic feather and the Simurg redeemed its promise
by saving her life.

Thus we find that the Simurg, like the Griffin, was
an intelligent creature who talked, and whose feathers had miraculous powers. A connection between
the two is still largely unproved, however.

The Griffin has a son, the Hippogriff, whose history is not nearly so hard to unravel. Appearing
rather late on the legendary scene, the Hippogriff en-
joyed its greatest adventures in the later Middle
Ages, although it had first appeared much earlier in
the Latin poetry of Virgil. While the Hippogriff's father was a Griffin, people said, its mother was a mare.
Like its sire, it had the head, forefeet, and wings of an
eagle, while its body, hind feet, and tail were like
those of a horse. The Hippogriff is not often mentioned in true folk tales, but it was very popular
among poets and the authors of allegories, to whom it
was a symbol of poetic inspiration. Its most famous
appearance is in Ariosto's great Italian narrative
poem *Orlando Furioso.* One part of the poem tells of
the wicked magician Atlantes, who used to ride out
on the Hippogriff to defend his magic castle. At last,
however, Atlantes was outwitted by his adversary,
Ruggiero. The Hippogriff then passed into the hands
of the hero Ruggiero, and together they had many
dazzling adventures. The Hippogriff was the perfect

steed for any hero—far ranging, untiring, and swifter than thought. One of its final exploits was to carry its master to the moon. At last, on the instructions of St. John the Evangelist, the Hippogriff was set free in the land of Provence, to roam at will through the clear Mediterranean skies.

Another winged wonder was Pegasus, the miraculous steed of Greek legend. The great flying horse was unique. Never was there a whole race of such creatures, only a single individual, marvelous beyond belief.

The winged steed of the Greeks was born from the blood of the Gorgon Medusa when she was slain by the hero Perseus, and his history shows us that he was a moon creature. Shining white as the moon in the night sky, he was beloved by the Muses, the nine mountain goddesses of poetic inspiration. For them Pegasus created the sacred spring called Hippocrene, striking it out from the earth with one stamp of his hoof. (It is because of the crescent-moon shape of their hoofs that horses have been linked to the moon goddess.)

Many years Pegasus roamed free on the blue slopes of the mountains and in the clear skies above them. Later, he was tamed by the prince Bellerophon, using a golden bridle that had been given him by the goddess Athena. Together, Bellerophon and Pegasus overcame the Chimaera, a fire-breathing monster shaped like a huge lion with a goat's head in the mid-

BELLEROPHON'S PEGASUS

dle of its back and a tail ending in the head of a
fanged serpent. The Chimaera is actually much older
than the Greek myth of Bellerophon. She dates back
to the period in Asia Minor (modern Turkey) when
the supreme ruler of the universe was considered to
be a goddess rather than a god. This goddess had
literally hundreds of names, but was recognized almost everywhere under the title of the Great Goddess. At the period when her worship prevailed in
Asia Minor, the year was divided into three seasons,
symbolized by the lion for spring, the goat for summer, and the snake for winter. The original Chimaera
was merely a joining of these three elements so that
they signified the whole year, to which was apparently added the breathing of fire because a well-
known volcano of the region was called Mount Chimaera.

Wonderful was the duel of Bellerophon and the
Chimaera. In imagination we can see the great horse
wheeling and plunging in the air, just out of reach of
fierce jaws, sharp horns, and fiery breath, while the
rider attacks with swift arrows and deadly spear. In
the end the hero is said to have downed the monster
by attaching a lump of lead to his spear and thrusting
it down her throat so that the lead melted and burned
her vitals. Afterward, Bellerophon and Pegasus
shared many other adventures, including the defeat
of the fierce Solymians and their allies the Amazons,
which was accomplished by flying above their heads

*Winged
Wonders*

and dropping boulders on them. The Solymians were followers of Salma, goddess of the spring equinox, and the Amazons were the warlike priestesses of the moon goddess. Thus it seems that in all his actions, from the taming of Pegasus on, Bellerophon represents a major change in the religious history of the area, when outside invaders brought in, and forced the people to accept, the worship of the sky father (most often called Zeus) in place of the Great Goddess. If we think back to the story of Marduk and Tiamat, the resemblances are obvious. World mythology contains thousands of similar stories, all describing in one way or another the conquest of goddess worshipers by those who followed the sky father or the marriage of god and goddess, indicating that the old religion had given way to the new but had not been entirely wiped out.

To return to Bellerophon, there is another, later chapter to the myth, which is not often told these days because it is not very flattering to human vanity. Bellerophon, it seems, was so puffed up with pride at his achievements that one day he mounted Pegasus and set off to join the gods in heaven. Up and up they soared, toward the summit of Mount Olympus, until Zeus punished the hero's presumption by sending a gadfly to sting Pegasus under the tail. The great steed reared, and Bellerophon was flung to earth. Pegasus now lives on Olympus, where he carries Zeus' thunderbolts. This part of the myth was very probably added by the worshipers of Zeus, who wanted to make sure no one missed the point that their god was greater than any mere sun hero.

Thus ended the legendary adventures of Pegasus, greatest of the flying horses of mythology. Joined to him in spirit, though not in breeding, are Sleipnir, the eight-legged steed upon whom the Norse god Odin rides the autumn wind; Enbarr, the horse of the Celtic Manannan Mac Lyr, "fleet as the naked cold wind of spring"; the Cloud-Horses of Java; the ember-red Smoke Horse of the Crow Indians; the Indian god Surya of the falcon's wings and gazelle's feet; and the Iranian god Tishtrya, who in the shape of a "white, beautiful horse, with golden ears and caparisoned in gold" did battle with the demon Apaosha, "a dark horse, bald with bald ears, bald with a bald back, bald with a bald tail, a frightful horse." Does it surprise you to learn that Apaosha is the demon of drought and Tishtrya is the Dog Star, here a type of Dragon, whose appearance in the night sky means the end of summer and the coming of the autumn rains? In mythology the same stories are told over and over, always changing, always the same.

SLEIPNIR,
HORSE OF THE WINDS

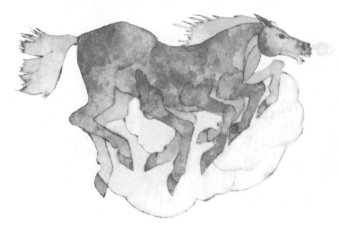

A School of VIII
Sea Monsters

Leviathan, that crooked serpent . . .
the dragon that is in the sea.
ISAIAH XXVII, I

I T is only fair to begin this chapter with a warning. When it comes to Sea Monsters, anything goes. For the Sea Serpent and its seagoing fellows are not simply the combination of myth and unnatural history that has operated to produce most of the beasts described in this book; they are also the subject of a very lively, complicated, modern argument that has ranged all the way from the scientific through the imaginative, the crankish, and the improbable to the deliberately fraudulent.

The problem of the Sea Monsters is complicated by the fact that everyone knows there are real monsters of the sea. The great oceans of this planet occupy about two thirds of the earth's surface and reach depths of thirty-six thousand feet, which is deeper than Mount Everest is high. The deepest parts of this undersea territory are virtually uncharted and unknown to us. In this ocean world live creatures that would be worthy to haunt any legend, pulled by strong and secret currents that we and the other land animals have long ago forgotten. The great whales, largest of living things, dwell in the ocean, as do the giant squids, and the sharks, those ancient and ruthless killers. There also are the harmless giants, the sunfish and the manta rays, and the lesser predators, the barracudas, the moray eels, the swordfishes. These and many more are the real monsters with whose presence we must reckon before we can properly assess the tales of strange sea creatures that appear in the folklore of almost every coastal nation.

One of the most ancient of such monsters was the Leviathan, which was once firmly believed in by every informed person because it is mentioned in the Book of Job: "Who can open the doors of his face? his teeth are terrible round about. His scales are his pride, shut up together as with a close seal. . . . Out of his mouth go burning lamps, and sparks of fire leap out. Out of his nostrils goeth smoke, as out of a seething pot or cauldron. . . . His heart is as firm as a stone; yea as firm as a piece of the nether millstone. When he raiseth himself up, the mighty are afraid. . . . The sword of him that layeth at him cannot hold; the spear, the dart, nor the habergeon. He esteemeth iron as straw, and brass as rotten wood. . . . He maketh the deep to boil like a pot. . . . Upon earth is not his like, who is made without fear."

In later times the Leviathan became the subject of much Jewish folklore. People said that it required a fish three miles long for its daily meal. It was also said that God, having created the first pair of Leviathans, repented of his action because they were so destructive. In his wisdom God destroyed one of the pair and made the other immortal, to serve humanity as an eternal reminder of the Creator's power and glory.

There was once much argument among scholars as to whether or not the Leviathan story was merely an exaggeration of reports concerning whales. Many maintain that it was, mainly on the grounds that the whale is the largest creature on earth, but there are some elements in the Leviathan's makeup that are most unwhalelike. For example, whales do not have scales of any sort, and most of the larger ones have only small teeth or none at all. Further, the breathing of fire is not characteristic of whales (though they do spout water vapor) so it would seem that the Leviathan must be at least distantly related to that old fire-breather the Dragon. However, as we mentioned in Chapter V, the word *Leviathan* is now interpreted as referring to the crocodile, and we saw in Chapters I and II that the crocodile was an important "ancestor" of the Dragon.

In the legends of Scandinavia there appears a monster somewhat like the Leviathan. It is the Kraken, whose principal characteristic is its incredible size. There are no accounts of its shape or features for the simple reason that it would require a team of mapmakers to put together an overall view of it. So big is the Kraken that when it rises to the surface of the sea to bask in the sun, unwary sailors may mistake it for an island. Weary of long months at sea, the men land on the unknown shore to stretch their legs and light a fire for cooking. Then the Kraken, not liking to have its skin used as a hearth, allows itself to sink beneath the waves, by which means many stout seamen have been drowned.

However, the Kraken has a healthy respect for saints and other members of the clergy. It is said that once a bishop, being on a sea voyage, sighted an island about a mile and a half in circumference which did not appear on the charts. Thinking to claim new territory for the Church, he had himself rowed ashore and celebrated a Mass. Only after the good church-man was safely back on board did the Kraken per-form its usual sinking trick.

Although it is generally a menace to navigation and a booby trap for sailors, the Kraken is often indirectly helpful to fishermen, for when it begins its rise from the ocean floor, large schools of fish are forced up-ward also. If their soundings tell them that the ocean is becoming shallower beneath them, the men quickly throw out their nets and prepare for a rich haul. Only, they must take care not to be greedy and linger too long, or they may be stranded on the back of the rising monster.

As with the Leviathan, the number of Krakens in the world is limited. Some say there are two, some that there is only one. There is a version of the leg-end that says the Kraken sleeps on the sea bottom and will remain there, in the words of the poet Tennyson, "until the latter fire shall heat the deep; then once by men and angels to be seen, in roaring he shall rise and on the surface die."

In looking for the source of the Kraken stories we find that the "ancestor" of the Kraken is probably the giant squid, a creature that was for years dismissed by naturalists as imaginary. It was only in the nineteenth century that the existence of this large relative of the octopus was proved to the satisfaction of scientists. Since members of this species have been known to reach eighty feet or more in length, they are pretty monstrous without the embellishments of legend. Add to this the fact that like other squids it sometimes floats with its flattish diamond-shaped body half awash, as if it were a sandbar. Finally, the Kraken, in its fiercer moods, is credited with the ability to snatch men from their ships with its long arms. While giant squids have not been proved to have this sinister habit, the sight of their waving tentacles is certainly enough to suggest that they might do such a thing.

If the Kraken is in truth to be traced to the giant squid, we may say that it belongs to the same order of creatures as a monster of classical legend, the Hydra. This horror lived in the Lernean swamps and was slain by the hero Hercules. The Hydra had nine snakelike heads, the ninth of which was supposed to be immortal, and a bad reputation as a bringer of plagues and other blights. Ancient carvings of the Hydra make it plain that the animal intended was a large octopus, whose eight tentacles might easily be mistaken for snakes' heads. The ninth, immortal head, was, of course, the octopus' real head, the one that had to be pierced before the creature could be killed. This arose from the fact that the octopus, like many of the lower animals, seems relatively unaffected by the loss of one of its limbs and may even grow replacements for the missing parts.

Though Hercules slew the Hydra once and for all, its distant relative, the Great Sea Serpent, has refused to die even yet. Alone in this age of doubters and debunkers, it has hung on in the face of assaults as determined as those St. George launched against his Dragon.

The Sea Serpent is not at all easy to describe, mainly because we do not know whether all the accounts refer to the same creature. The only points on which all agree are that it is enormously long and generally snaky in appearance, and that it swims very fast, with its head and several feet of neck out of water. It may live anywhere in the seven seas and its history goes back as far as the first fragile man-made boats that dared to cross a piece of open ocean.

One of the earliest appearances of the Sea Serpent in myth occurs among Norse and Teutonic tales. Jormungandr, they say, is the great serpent that lies at the bottom of the ocean. It is of such length that it encircles the earth, and, like the Kraken, it will not rise to the surface until the end of the world. On that day it will thrash its great coils over the earth and destroy all mankind.

Among historical accounts of the Sea Serpent the first may be Aristotle's. In the fourth century B.C. the great Greek scientist told of large seagoing serpents that lived near the coast of Libya, stealing oxen for food and attacking passing ships. Other classical authors who mention the Serpent are the historian Livy and the naturalist Pliny, who gives the length of the monster as a relatively small thirty feet.

In later centuries the Sea Serpent quite outgrew these modest beginnings. Conrad Gesner, the sixteenth-century author of a widely read book on animals, included a picture of a Sea Serpent that he stated to be six hundred feet long. Gesner's Serpent was an especially fierce one. It was shown attacking a full-rigged sailing vessel, crushing it in the segmented coils of its monstrous body.

Six hundred feet was about the top limit of length claimed for any Sea Serpent. By the time Gesner's book was published, explorers were already bringing back reports of new worlds across the ocean. Educated people had known for centuries that the earth was round, and it was becoming clear, even to the most ignorant common sailor, that the edges of the until-then known world were not filled with whirlpools, tornadoes, and nameless monsters. Only the mapmakers, wishing to fill up the empty spaces showing uncharted seas, continued to draw strange creatures with an assortment of fins, flippers, feelers, tentacles, and tusks.

In the ordinary course of unnatural history the sixteenth and seventeenth centuries should have marked the end of the Sea Serpent's career. All kinds of superstitions and legends were being discredited, as people learned to rely on their own observation for their judgments, instead of on hearsay. Yet strangely enough, tales of the Sea Serpent became not fewer but more numerous during the years between 1700 and the present. From every part of the world ships sent reports of having sighted long, snakelike Somethings. Generally, these reports were laughed at by professors, reporters, and other experts. Often, they had good reason to laugh, for there are large numbers of things that can be mistaken for Sea Serpents unless the person doing the looking is very careful. It is certainly true, as many have shown, that some observers were seeing floating logs, half-submerged wrecks, whales, lines of swimming seals or porpoises, mats of seaweed, waterspouts, lines of low-flying birds, reflections of nearby objects, mirages, or other optical illusions. In addition, judging the size of a thing seen at sea is notoriously difficult, because there are no features of the landscape with which to compare them. Thus a normal-size sea snake, oarfish, or pipefish could easily be mistaken by a novice for a much larger creature especially when the observer is looking down into clear water from the deck of a ship.

One must also consider the fact that over the centuries the Sea Serpent and other Sea Monsters have been favorite subjects for hoaxes ranging from the

A School of Sea Monsters

amusing to the criminal. During the sixteenth and seventeenth centuries, the manufacture of fake monsters of various sorts reached the proportions of an industry in many coastal regions. Using dried parts from skates, rays, and a variety of other creatures, it was possible to create very lifelike "specimens" which could then be sold to the curious public at high prices. For some unknown reason these little works of art were known in English as Jenny Hanivers. They were often represented to the buyer as being the young of some huge monster of the deep, and thus helped to confuse the issue for centuries.

The Sea Serpent was also the star of several large-scale frauds which were a good deal less innocent. In 1845 a Dr. Albert C. Koch announced that he was about to exhibit the skeleton of a genuine Sea Serpent on Broadway in New York City. People flocked to see the marvel, which did indeed resemble a serpent, being over a hundred feet long and having frightful beaklike jaws. Unfortunately, the bones which Dr. Koch had strung together so cleverly belonged not to a living Sea Serpent but to an extinct whale called *Zeuglodon.* The ambitious showman made a handsome profit on his investment before he was found out. It is certainly not hard to see why many people came to regard any talk of the Sea Serpent with doubt, if not with outright scorn.

But still—still, there is something about the evidence that continues to attract the attention of reliable scholars, in spite of the lack of decisive proof, in spite of the frauds and hoaxes. Out of all the reports and rumors, a few cases remain that do not seem explainable in terms of any known animal or object. Instead, there begins to emerge some sort of consistent picture of the Sea Serpent, or rather, the Sea Serpents. For if one is to take the subject at all seriously, it soon becomes clear that there are at least two creatures to which the accounts refer.

The first we may call for the sake of clarity the Maned Sea Serpent, earliest and in some ways best described by Archbishop Olaus Magnus, a native of Sweden. In 1555 he wrote of a creature often seen by Scandinavian sailors. "He hath commonly hair hanging from his neck a Cubit long, and sharp scales, and is black, and he hath flaming shining eyes. This snake disquiets the Shippers, and he puts his head high like a pillar, and catcheth away men, and he devours them." It is unfortunate that the Archbishop strains our powers of belief by adding that the creature is commonly two hundred feet long and twenty feet thick. (The largest whale on record was just over one hundred thirteen feet.) However, the Maned Sea Serpent soon made its appearance again.

This time the witness was Lorenz von Ferry, a Norwegian who held the impressive title of royal commander and pilot general at Bergen. Von Ferry and others swore in a court of law that they had sighted, in August of 1746, a monster whose head "resembled that of a horse." It was grayish, they said, and had "large black eyes and a long white mane, which hung down to the surface of the water."

Among the many later performances of the Maned Sea Serpent, the most famous by far occurred on Oc-

MANED SEA SERPENT

A School of Sea Monsters

HUMPED SEA SERPENT

tober 11, 1848. On that day Captain Peter M'Quhae and six members of the crew of his ship HMS *Daedalus* sighted a most unusual creature swimming near the vessel. Everyone who saw it agreed that it was "an enormous serpent, with head and shoulders kept about four feet constantly above the surface of the sea. . . . Its color [was] a dark brown, with yellowish white about the throat. It had no fins, but something like a màne of a horse, or rather a bunch of seaweed, washed about its back." The report adds that the animal's length was about sixty feet, its diameter behind the head about sixteen inches, and that it was in full view for twenty minutes in conditions of good visibility.

Following the sighting from the *Daedalus,* many ingenious explanations were advanced. If you think it likely that seven experienced and reputable seamen spent twenty minutes staring in awe at an ordinary sea lion, or that they concocted a hoax and kept the secret all their lives long, then you may belong to the camp of the scoffers. Personally, I hold the view that no satisfactory explanation has yet been put forward, although one may someday be found. In any case, whether it be fictitious or not, the Maned Sea Serpent is surely entitled to a good laugh at the confusion it has caused in the human world.

In the case of the Maned Sea Serpent's cousin the Humped Sea Serpent, the good laugh may well become a hysterical fit. This second monster found its

way into history and out of legend in July 1734, when it was spied by a Norwegian missionary named Hans Egede off the shore of Greenland. Egede later wrote out an apparently sober and objective account of the happening, which states in part that the animal "raised itself so high above the water, that its head reached above our maintop. It had a long, sharp snout, and blew like a whale, had broad, large flappers, and the body was, as it were, covered with a hard skin, and it was very wrinkled and uneven on its skin; moreover, on the lower part it was formed like a snake, and when it went under water again, it cast itself backwards, and in doing so it raised its tail above the water, a whole ship-length from its body."

There have been many later sightings of this or a similar creature, all of which are striking in that they emphasize that the body is thicker than either head or tail. One of the most typical of these appearances occurred in the harbor of the picturesque fishing village of Gloucester, Massachusetts, in 1817, the month being August (a favorite month for Sea Serpents). An eminent scientific society later published an account of the happening that included these remarks about the creature: "It was said to resemble a serpent in its general form and motions, to be of immense size, and to move with wonderful rapidity; to appear on the surface of the water only in calm and bright weather; and to seem jointed or like a number of buoys or casks following each other in a line." The animal, whatever it was, remained in Gloucester harbor from August tenth to August twenty-third and seemed to be of a playful nature. It paid no attention to boats or human observers, but appeared to enjoy looping itself about in the water and generally displaying itself to the best advantage. It showed no desire whatever to devour sailors or ravage the coastline. All these facts were collected in a long report and vouched for by many independent witnesses.

But if the first chapter in the history of the Humped Sea Serpent of Gloucester is soberly scientific, the second is purest farce. Like so many of the family, the Gloucester Sea Serpent was the victim of scientific humbug. About a month after the Serpent's departure, a boy found a small black snake on a beach not far from Gloucester. Somehow the rumor sprang up that the Sea Serpent had laid eggs on the shore and that this was one of its young. Fortunately (or perhaps not so fortunately), the snake was sent to the investigating committee of the scientific society that had reported on the original Serpent. The little thing was solemnly dissected and pronounced to be a genuine Sea Serpent, mainly because it had a series of lumps on its back like those reported on its supposed parent. Everyone concerned was delighted. It was really a pity that Henri Ducrotay de Blainville, an eminent French zoologist, declared the following year that the "specimen" was in reality an ordinary, though slightly malformed, young blacksnake of the kind found all over North America.

Thus the Sea Serpent officially slipped back into the land of legend. Anyone nowadays who reports seeing a standard Sea Serpent, Humped, Maned, or otherwise, is sure to be laughed at. Yet still the reports come in—from the seven seas, from Lake Chad in central Africa, from Lake Baikal in the USSR, from Lake Champlain on the United States-Canadian border (where the creature is called "Champie"), from Florida's St. Johns River (home of an alleged something known as "Pinkie"), from a variety of lakes and lochs in Ireland and Scandinavia, and of course from Loch Ness, Scotland (see Chapter IX). And there are still researchers who have kept the issue alive. Among them Belgian zoologist Bernard Heuvelmans has written a six-hundred-page book entitled *In the Wake of the Sea-Serpents* in which he proposes that reports of sightings actually refer to no fewer than *nine* separate kinds of large sea animals, which he calls, respectively, the Father-of-all-the-Turtles, the Long-necked Sea-Serpent, the Merhorse, the Many-finned Sea-Serpent, the Marine Saurian (that is, lizard), the Super-eel, the Super-otter, and the Yellow-belly. The plain fact is that no one can say definitely whether one or more genuine monsters of the sea, members of hitherto unknown species, do in fact live and breed in the unexplored depths of the sea. What is needed is some sort of giant aquarium, a vast Sea Serpent trap that can be erected around an area in which the Great Unknown has been sighted. Then the scientists, the underwater explorers, the skeptics, and the believers could all get together and make a decisive search to determine whether the last supposed monster is after all a reality.

Astonishingly enough, something like the giant aquarium described above does exist, and the story of what goes on, or may go on, in it is contained in the next chapter. For Loch Ness, Scotland, may be, and ought to be, a laboratory ready-made for those who would like to learn the truth about at least one form of Sea Serpent.

A JENNY HANIVER

A School of
Sea Monsters

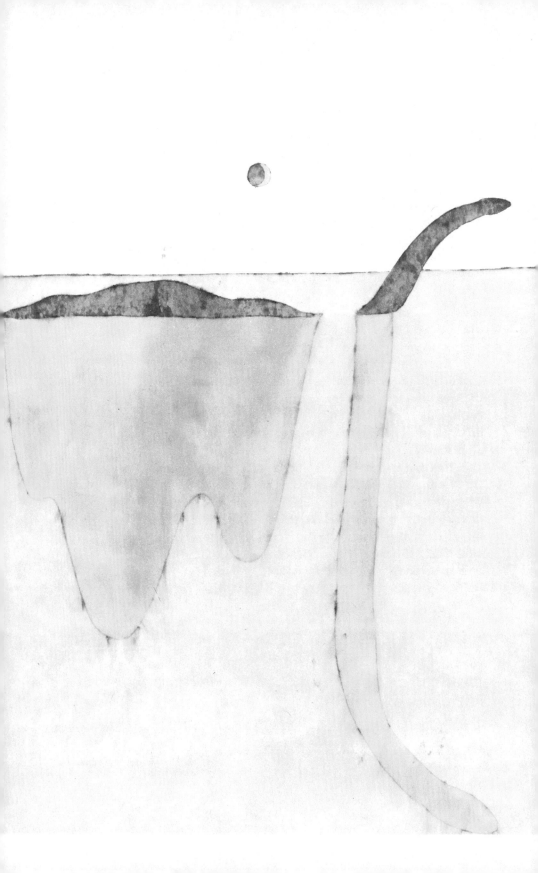

Loch Ness: Last Laugh?　　　IX

*There are more things in heaven
and earth, Horatio, than are
dreamt of in your philosophy.*
SHAKESPEARE

O N E day, about fourteen hundred years ago, a man
was walking by the bleak shores of Loch Ness. He
was St. Columba, an Irish missionary who had been
sent to convert the pagan Scots. Not far off, a swimmer was churning his way to shore. Suddenly the
saint saw that the man was not alone in the water. A
great head and neck had reared themselves from the
waves and were hanging over the unwary swimmer.
St. Columba was a man of action. Raising his crucifix
in the air, he stepped to the water's edge and shouted
across at the monster, "Halt! Go thou hence, nor
trouble more this man!" The monster respected the
man of God and, so the legend says, the long snaky

neck bowed in submission and sank slowly beneath the surface of the loch.

At that time Scotland was a barbaric land almost unknown to the more civilized inhabitants of southern Europe. Then, as now, Loch Ness was a body of fresh water stretching a twenty-four-mile-long finger diagonally across the northern part of the land along a line from the Firth of Lorne to the Moray Firth, and connected to those branches of the sea only by shallower waterways. Since St. Columba's day tales of something unusual in the Loch have appeared at intervals, right up to the present. The press and popular writers have christened the phenomenon Nessie, but the nickname is misleading, since it suggests that there is only one creature in the Loch, although it is obviously nonsense that any single beast could be responsible for fourteen hundred years of sighting reports. If the loch is home to anything unusual at all, there must be a breeding population large enough to replace itself periodically. Thus it seems more logical to refer to plural monsters rather than a single Nessie.

The career of the monsters in the twentieth century begins in 1933, when a series of people reported seeing a group of humps moving across the water. Sometimes the humps were accompanied by a long neck with a small turtlelike head that peered about curiously. On one occasion a monster was reported on land in full daylight. The witnesses were Mr. and Mrs. G. Spicer, who reported that an astonishing creature had crossed the road in front of their car. It had a thick body very close to or on the ground, no visible legs, and a long wavy neck. The Spicers were so startled that they failed to notice what sort of head the thing had, but they did recall that it was dirty gray and moved over the ground in a series of jerks.

A few months later a Mr. Arthur Grant again saw the beast on land and was able to observe something of the head, which he described as like that of an eel. He said that the animal had flippers and a rounded tail, and was about eighteen feet long.

This, one begins to feel, is monster hunting as it should be. The quarry is more or less trapped in its landlocked home, it has been sighted many times, and, finally, it has been spotted on land, where the whole animal was visible at once. Too, the loch is a favorable place for a monster refuge, being about 750 feet deep in some places, and stocked with enough fish to support quite a few large creatures.

But there is still more evidence that must be considered in this case, for the development of the camera in the last century has given modern monster-hunters a superb new weapon. By luck or design several photographs have been taken of the Monster, and one—a 16mm motion picture made in 1960—was turned over to the British Royal Air Force for analysis. The RAF is expert in examining photographs made for the purpose of military or geographical reconnaissance, many of which are taken at night, at high altitudes, or under other difficult conditions. *The New York Times* of February 21, 1966, carried a report of the RAF investigators' conclusions. First, the film showed some living creature moving through the waters of the loch. It was not a shadow on the water, not a stationary snag or floating log, not even a speedboat. Furthermore, the panel stated, the thing pictured was about ninety-two feet long and six feet wide, and was moving at a rate of ten miles per hour. And, finally, there was no evidence that the photograph was a deliberate fake. Altogether, the Monster had not been given such a boost for several decades.

But, of course, the *Times* report was far from proof that a "monster" inhabits the loch, or even that there was anything there at all. Groups of experts have been wrong before, as we saw in the case of the "baby Sea Serpent" of Gloucester.

During the next several summers the loch became one of the busiest places in Scotland. An organization called the Loch Ness Investigation Bureau acquired semipermanent quarters near the loch and began an ambitious program of keeping Urquhart Bay (a particularly active spot for monster sightings) under constant observation during the warm-weather months. Boats carrying monster seekers patrolled the waters, cameras at the ready, and there was even an attempt to chase after the monster in a miniature submarine. (The loch's waters were so murky, however, that little could be seen at distances over a few feet.)

So much fuss was made that the British Parliament became concerned for the safety of Scotland's shy resident, and in 1975 the beast was given the scientific name *Nessiteras rhombopteryx* so that it could come under a British law protecting rare animals. (The Greek name, translated, means "Ness-wonder," or "Ness monster, with diamond-shaped flippers.")

Probably the most prominent figure in this whole scene was Robert Rines, an attorney who in 1963 founded the Academy of Applied Science and later used its facilities in pursuit of his fascination with the monster. As a result of the efforts of Rines and others, several different kinds of modern technology were brought to bear on the problem. Underwater cameras were suspended in the loch and attached to electronic triggering devices that would trip shutters and strobe lights at the same moment, whenever sonar information gave evidence that large bodies were moving about in the waters nearby. (Sonar is a method for "seeing" objects by bouncing sound waves off them, in much the same way that bats and whales navigate in the dark.) And, to avoid the problem of sitting still while waiting for a monster to come to the camera, a side-scan sonar rig with printed readout was repeatedly towed through the Loch in an effort to spot monsters outside Urquhart Bay. Attempts were also made to attract monsters by means of fish oil and recordings of the sounds made by schools of salmon, presumed to be the beasts' chief source of food. One investigator even proposed to build an underwater cage or trap, but was prevented by others who argued that it would be wrong to risk killing or injuring an animal so rare, mysterious, and presumably endangered.

And what was the result of all this expenditure of time, money, effort, and printer's ink? On the one hand, not nearly enough to satisfy skeptical scientists that *Nessiteras rhombopteryx* was any more real than the Brollachan or the Nuckelavee. On the other, at least three pieces of interesting and controversial evidence. The first is a pair of photographs taken by the underwater camera in 1972. They show, in blotchy black and white, a single diamond-shaped something, quite like a flapper, and apparently attached to a large body that nearly fills the camera frame. Rines and his supporters interpret these photos as showing one of those rhomboidal limbs from which the monsters got their name, and evidence from the observers' records can be used to infer that the flapper was about six feet long. Next, in 1975, Rines and his colleagues obtained an alleged body shot of a monster, apparently swimming up and into the left part of the camera frame from bottom right. What is suggested, rather hazily, is the upper half of a body and long, up-curving neck, with the light source on the right highlighting at least one fin or flapper. Absolutely no detail is visible, and the left-hand half of the "body" is in deep shadow. Finally, there is the sensational 1975 "head shot," which was taken at a time when the underwater camera was so heavily disturbed that it swung upward and also photographed the hull of the boat from which it hung. This shot, if it indeed shows a monster, is both alarming and startling, for the supposed head is blunt-nosed, ridged, and pitted, in a way that makes one think as much of a crab as of a reptile. However interesting it may be, it cannot help puzzling us, since visual reports of the monster hardly even mention the head, implying that it is small and featureless—certainly nothing like this craggy and crusty protuberance. Even the conclusion that the object is indeed a head is not all that obvious, since neither eyes nor mouth can be easily identified.

In addition to these three star exhibits, there are several sonar tracings from 1976 that indicate largish objects moving through the loch's waters, and one that shows something about thirty feet long, with a bodylike bulge between elongated "head" and "tail" at rest on the bottom in three hundred feet of water.

These items are certainly something, but they are not all one can expect. Scientists and tourists have spent thousands of hours peering after monsters in the last decade, and have nothing decisive to show for it. There are actually only three possibilities in the case. Perhaps there *is* a population of large, unknown animals living in the loch (and maybe in other northern lakes from Scandinavia to Russia to North America, which have been the sources of similar reports), and these are authentic, though confused, evidence of their existence. Or, Rines and perhaps his colleagues may be guilty of a hoax, although it must be said that the conspiracy would have to be a fairly large one and there is much truth in the saying that three can keep a secret if two of them are dead. Or, finally, there may be no hoax, but the evidence may be misleading. The best any of us can do is examine the evidence and judge for ourselves. (Roy Mackal's *The Monsters of Loch Ness,* as listed under "Some References" in the back of this book, is probably the best single source, although I am not convinced by his thesis that the monsters are giant amphibians.)

One important supporter of the "misleading evidence" explanation is Robert P. Craig, who in 1982 published an article in a respected scientific journal, claiming that those who believed they had seen monsters had actually been deceived by—pine trees. Craig, a retired engineer, calculated that pines falling into the loch develop very considerable gas pressures inside them as a result of natural decay and the sealing effect of their own resins, and he suggests that the long "necks" of monsters are reported when someone sees one of these logs pop to the surface, propelled by its own escaping gases. It is an interesting idea, and one that could certainly explain some monster sightings, although it would hardly help us with evidence like the Dinsdale film or the underwater sonar tracings.

Let us accept, for the sake of argument, that there is some unknown living creature in Loch Ness. The next problem naturally is, what sort of creature? Is it mammal, reptile, amphibian, fish, or perhaps an invertebrate, one of the many species without a backbone? This question has been asked about Sea Serpents in general, and to some extent the answers may be taken to apply to both. It is necessary to remember, however, that the possible existence of the Loch Ness Monster proves nothing, one way or the other, about the existence of the Sea Serpent.

The most popular candidate for Loch Ness's strange inhabitant is a plesiosaur, one of a group of great sea reptiles that, as far as is known, has not been seen on earth since the Mesozoic Era. A plesiosaur would make a very good Sea Serpent, having a long neck, a humped back, flappers, and a long tail. Nor is it possible to prove that the creature could *not* have survived tens of millions of years after the death of the other giant reptiles. Yet the idea is unlikely.

Besides, there is another objection to the notion that the animal we are looking for is a reptile. All the living reptiles are cold blooded. This means that they find it very hard to survive prolonged cold, because they do not produce their own body heat as mammals and birds do. In temperate climates snakes and their kin generally hibernate during the winter. There is, however, no known example of a reptile that hibernates in the water, and it seems highly unlikely that during the severe Scottish winters the caves around Loch Ness are full of sleeping plesiosaurs.

In recent years, however, an exciting new idea about dinosaurs has been put forward, and it is one that could be of great significance for monster lovers. Some scientists (a small but vigorous minority) now believe that certain groups of dinosaurs (as distinct from reptiles in general) may have been warm blooded. If there are unknown creatures surviving in the cold depths of Loch Ness and other northern lakes, it would certainly help them to be warm blooded, though they would have to eat enormous amounts of food.

Perhaps, if the monster is not a dinosaur/reptile, it is a mammal. Seagoing mammals such as the whale and the seal thrive in cold climates, and the Sea Serpent of the open ocean may be a long, thin beast like the extinct *Zeuglodon,* a sort of giraffe among whales. This might help to explain a humped animal with flippers, like that seen by Hans Egede, but whales are conspicuous spouters and given to traveling in herds, characteristics that seem most unsuitable for the apparently shy and solitary dwellers in Loch Ness.

Supposing the monster to be a mammal, but not a whale, might it belong to the seal tribe? A seal of great size with a long neck would satisfy most requirements. But seals rear their young on land, and the babies are unable to swim at birth. Even in the unlikely event that such a seal might manage to migrate to some distant breeding ground, it seems strange its haunts have not been spotted by sailors or explorers. Seals are generally noisy animals, and since they breed in colonies which may number many thousands, one would think they would be rather hard to miss. To get around this difficulty some writers have suggested that the animal sighted in 1933 was only a large individual seal of some kind. But what then becomes of the earlier reports? Seals do not have a life span much over a few decades. Does

Loch Ness for some reason breed a succession of ordinary but oversize seals? That is almost harder to believe than all the other theories put together.

In 1956 Dr. Maurice Burton made a most intriguing proposal concerning the monster's identity. In the course of some research into the history of Loch Ness, Dr. Burton became interested in the family of the Anguillidae, or eels. These animals, which are technically bony fishes, are at the same time remarkable and mysterious. Eels are capable of great feats of endurance and have startling acrobatic powers. They can wriggle over sheer stone walls, travel over land for considerable distances, live in salt water or fresh, and occasionally dig in the ground. The so-called common eel of Europe lives in fresh water but returns to the sea to spawn. In most species of eel the eggs hatch into a larval form which later shrinks somewhat before becoming a juvenile eel. This last characteristic is responsible for much of the mystery surrounding the family, since the larval forms are not easy to identify with the appropriate adult eels, to which they may bear little or no resemblance. In other words, there may be known larval eels whose full-grown forms have not yet been discovered. It is an established fact that adult eels ten feet long may grow from larvae of five inches. What, then, might be the size of the adult eel that was due to grow from the six-*foot* larva captured at sea in 1930 by Dr. Anton Bruun of the Woods Hole Oceanographic Institute?

Dr. Burton cited other facts about eels in support

of his theory. The eel's rate of growth is much greater in northern locations, such as Loch Ness, and in enclosed waters. Second, in an enclosed group of eels, some will feed off the smaller ones and thus attain a greatly increased rate of growth. Third, from the studies of various oceangoing eels such as the moray and the conger, it is clear that some individual eels grow far above the average size, for, unlike mammals, fish may continue to grow almost indefinitely.

As a final fillip to his argument, Dr. Burton adds that he has observed on two occasions an eel swimming rapidly on its side. This is important, since an eel usually swims with its narrow edge upward in the water, as if it were a picket fence. In that position it is impossible for it to produce those moving humps which are so characteristic of many Sea Serpent stories. On the other hand, an eel swimming on its side would look not like the sideways waves of a picket fence but like the up-and-down humps of a roller coaster. Certainly the eel has in its favor the fact that it survives well in cold climates and need not surface to breathe.

We should also consider the possibility that the monster is not an animal with a backbone at all, but one of the invertebrates. At least one authority has recently suggested that a giant form of sea slug (a shell-less relative of the snail) may be responsible for the sightings. Up to the present time, however, this idea has not received widespread support.

There is just one more view of the Loch Ness Monster which we must consider, and, like the others, it applies in general to Sea Serpent lore. It is the belief that all the people who have reported seeing the Monster have been suffering from some sort of hallucination. In other words, what they saw had no existence outside their own minds, though they may have been honest in reporting their impressions. It is not fair to laugh at this notion without thought, for it is certainly true that people tend to see what they expect at any given time. If you have been warned that a house is haunted, a flutter of white may send you screaming out the door, whereas at other times you might merely wonder why someone had left a sheet draped over the banister. (This, of course, is assuming you believe in ghosts, at least a little.) In any case, it is only right for us to remember that in this century most who reported seeing the monster had heard of it before. Each person must decide whether so many witnesses could have been deluded in the same way and whether the photographs represent honest error, deliberate fraud, or actual reality.

It is interesting to note that today we are in the same position as the people of a hundred fifty years ago. Then, it was the existence of the Unicorn that was in question. A little sadly, the Unicorn turned out to be nothing but legend. It is now as dead as the dodo bird, the one having been killed by human curiosity, the other by human carelessness. How lucky we are that we still live in an age in which there is room for doubt about at least one monster—where the possibility and the challenge still exist. Will the Sea Serpent at the last be ranked with the Unicorn or with the salamander? Like all our ancestors before us, we must admit there are some questions we haven't answered. Ours is still the privilege of wondering.

*Today
is not yet*
THE END

SOME REFERENCES

Barbeau, Marius. *The Golden Phoenix,* and Other French-Canadian Fairy Tales. New York: Henry Z. Walck, 1958.

Baring-Gould, Sabine *Curious Myths of the Middle Ages.* New Hyde Park, N.Y.: University Books, 1967.

Baring-Gould, William S., and Cecil Baring-Gould, eds. *The Annotated Mother Goose.* New York: Clarkson N. Potter, 1962.

Barrett, Charles. *The Bunyip, and Other Mythical Monsters and Legends.* Melbourne: Reed & Harris, 1946.

Botkin, B. A., ed. *A Treasury of American Folklore.* New York: Crown Publishers, 1944.

Briggs, Katharine. *An Encyclopedia of Fairies: Hobgoblins, Brownies, Bogies, and other Supernatural Creatures.* New York: Pantheon Books, 1976.

Burton, Maurice. *Animal Legends.* New York: Coward-McCann, Inc., 1957.

Campbell, Joseph. *The Masks of God.* New York: Viking Press, 1956, 1962, 1964, 1968. 4 volumes.

Carpenter, Frances. *Wonder Tales of Horses and Heroes.* Garden City, New York: Doubleday & Co., 1952.

Carrington, Richard. *Mermaids and Mastodons: A Book of Natural and Unnatural History.* New York: Rinehart & Co., 1957.

Curtin, Jeremiah. *Fairy Tales of Eastern Europe.* New York: Medill McBride Co., 1949.

Fenner, Phyllis. *Giants and Witches and a Dragon or Two.* New York: Alfred A. Knopf, 1954.

Frazer, Sir James. *The New Golden Bough,* abridged edition by Theodor H. Gastner. Great Meadows, New Jersey: S. G. Phillips, Inc., 1959.

Gesner, Conrad. *Historia Animalium.* Basel: 1551.

Gould, Charles. *Mythical Monsters.* London: W.H. Allen & Co., 1886.

Graves, Robert. *The Greek Myths.* New York: Penguin Books, 1966.

Graves, Robert. *The White Goddess: A Historical Grammar of*

Poetic Myth. New York: American Book–Stratford Press, Inc., 1948.

Gray, Louis Herbert, ed. The *Mythology of All Races.* New York: Cooper Square, 1964. 13 volumes.

Grimm, Jacob and Wilhelm. *Fairy Tales,* ed. Elenore Abbot. New York: Charles Scribner's Sons, 1947.

Heuvelmans, Bernard. *In the Wake of the Sea-Serpents.* New York: Hill and Wang, 1968.

Heuvelmans, Bernard. *On the Track of Unknown Animals.* New York: Paladin Books, 1965.

Howey, M. Oldfield. *The Horse in Magic and Myth.* London: William Rider, 1923.

Ingersoll, Ernest. *Dragons and Dragon Lore.* New York: Payson & Clarke, Ltd., 1928.

Jobes, Gertrude. *Dictionary of Mythology, Folklore, and Symbols.* New York: Scarecrow Press, 1962. 3 volumes.

Lang, Andrew. *The Crimson Fairy Book.* New York: Longmans, Green & Co., 1947.

Lewinsohn, Richard. *Animals, Men and Myths,* translated from the German. New York: Harper & Brothers, 1954.

Ley, Willy. *Exotic Zoology.* New York: Viking Press, 1959.

Lum, Peter. *Fabulous Beasts.* New York: Pantheon, 1951.

MacDonnell, Anne. *The Italian Fairy Book.* London: Unwin, Ltd., 1911.

Mackal, Roy. *The Monsters of Loch Ness.* Chicago: Swallow Press, 1976.

The New Larousse Encyclopedia of Mythology. New York: Bonanza Books, 1968.

Scott-Stokes, H.F. *Perseus: Of Dragons.* London: Kegan Paul, Trench Trubner & Co., 1924.

Shepard, Odell. *The Lore of the Unicorn.* New York: Houghton Mifflin, 1930.

Soule, Gardner. *The Maybe Monsters.* New York: G.P. Putnam's Sons, 1963.

Steel, Flora Annie. *English Fairy Tales.* New York: Macmillan, 1918.

Wendt, Herbert. trans. Michael Bullock. *Out of Noah's Ark: The Story of Man's Discovery of the Animal Kingdom.* Boston: Houghton Mifflin, 1959.

Werner, E.T. Chalmers. *Myths and Legends of China.* London: Harrap, 1922.

White, T.H., trans. and ed. *Bestiary. The Book of Beasts.* New York: Capricorn Books, G.P. Putnam's Sons, 1960.

INDEX

Index

• • • • • • •

118